Jesus in bad company

Adolf Holl

Jesus in bad company

translated from the German by
Simon King

Holt, Rinehart and Winston
New York   Chicago   San Francisco

For I.S.

Jesus in schlechter Gesellschaft
was first published in Germany in 1971

Copyright © 1971 Deutsche Verlags-Anstalt
GmbH, Stuttgart
English translation © 1972 by William Collins
Sons & Co. Ltd., London and Holt, Rinehart
and Winston, Inc., New York

Published simultaneously in Canada by Holt,
Rinehart and Winston of Canada, Limited.

ISBN: 0-03-0013860

Library of Congress Catalog Card Number: 72-78146

First published in the U.S. in 1973
Printed in the United States of America

232
H

Contents

Contents

Jesus in bad company

Chapter 1

An amazing life story

Jesus's birth is placed a few years before Christ because a medieval calendarist made a mistake.[1] In the light of modern knowledge, his birth can be dated between four and six years BC, and that, together with his execution about AD 30, is just about the only biographical detail on which the experts are able to agree.

Some learned men even dispute the fact that Jesus ever lived, seeing him instead as a mythical figure.[2] But such men aside, there are about a thousand million people today who pray to him, which is to say that approximately one third of the world's population calls itself Christian.

Jesus's public ministry lasted at most for three years, probably only for two, and quite possibly for just a few months. Of what happened before, almost nothing is said in the sources on which we exclusively depend, namely the 'gospels' of Matthew, Mark, Luke, and John. It is true that Matthew and Luke supply us with some information about the miraculous circumstances surrounding the birth of the divine child at Bethlehem, but our interest in more precise biographical detail remains unsatisfied.

It is as though Jesus suddenly appeared as a mature man: 'then Jesus came from Galilee to the Jordan to John, to be baptized by him' (Matthew and Mark); 'Jesus, when he began his ministry, was about thirty years of age, being the son (as was supposed) of Joseph' (Luke); 'the next day he [the Baptist] saw Jesus coming toward him' (John).[3]

In this context, only John's account actually names a place: these things, he says, were done in Bethany, beyond the Jordan. It was, then, to that place, somewhere not too far from where the Jordan flows into the Dead Sea and quite close to the old city of Jericho, that Jesus seems to have gone in order to receive his penitential baptism at the hands of John. Shortly afterwards people began to talk about Jesus. But the one question that inevitably springs to mind – 'How is it that this man has learning, when he has never studied?'[4] – remains unanswered in the gospel accounts.

AN UNKNOWN PAST

The information-gap between the childhood accounts and Jesus's emergence before the public gaze is considerable. In effect, only Luke breaks the silence, and then only once: 'Now his parents went to Jerusalem every year at the feast of the Passover. And when he was twelve years old, they went up according to custom.'

The story[5] tells us that, unknown to his parents, Jesus lingered with the 'doctors' in the temple, astonishing them with his knowledge and with his answers to their questions. But his parents discovered him there and he returned with them obediently to Nazareth where he 'increased in wisdom and in stature, and in favour with God and man'.

Even Luke felt no need to report more than this. It appears that his basic concern was to make it clear to his readers that Jesus had no need for schooling. His knowledge of the Jewish writings, and his ability to read and write, he must, therefore, have picked up elsewhere: from 'above'; that is, from God.

But this account by no means closes the information-gap, for what it offers is not information but instead a miraculous explanation for the fact, apparently taken for granted by Luke, that Jesus was familiar with the Scriptures.

That this was indeed the case seems very probable. Jesus was often addressed as 'Rabbi', which is like calling someone 'Master'. But a rabbi in those days would have had a long and thorough education behind him. Normally a man would have studied for some twenty to thirty years, starting as a child, before he was entitled to call himself a teacher. Jewish society was among the first in those days to develop a highly educated upper class[6] and the rigorous grounding required of its rabbis must be understood in this context.

However, it is not claimed at any point that Jesus belonged to the leading group of those well versed in the Scriptures; on the contrary, he stood in sharp opposition to them, particularly to one of the dominant schools – the Pharisees, whom he accused of hypocrisy. The same charge is made against the Pharisees by the writers of the Qumran scrolls – the first of which came to light in 1947. Qumran is not very far from the district in which according to tradition Jesus first preached. May we suppose that Jesus himself belonged to the Essenes, the desert brotherhood which at that time was active on the north-west bank of the Dead Sea, and whose customs and doctrines are reported in the Qumran texts? Is it possible that it was at their hands that Jesus obtained the education that enabled him to make such confident use of the sacred books?[7]

We don't know. The question of Jesus's scholastic and vocational education remains unanswered.

Neither do we know anything about his marital status. Did he marry, or not? Tradition couldn't tolerate the notion of a married Jesus, though today people are prepared to consider the possibility.[8] Here, too, the gospels tell us nothing at all. Some would say that the gospels say nothing about Jesus being married for the very good reason that he wasn't. But to draw conclusions from silence is a method that historians rightly reject. Anyway, one could equally well argue the reverse: a married Jesus who left his wife so as to dedicate himself exclusively to his mission. Gospel silence on this point could then be explained on the grounds either that the evangelists were indifferent on this point, or that they chose to repress information about a marriage, considering such an event to be contrary to their interests.

We have nothing to go by but silence and conjecture, and we know well enough that in the absence of reliable information a supposition in whatever direction can never harden into truth.

Whether, in Mark's account, it is Joseph or Jesus himself who originally was described as a carpenter is not sufficiently clear from the text. Scholars nowadays are unsure and prefer to leave a question mark where others picture the holy family – the growing boy at Joseph's side in the Nazareth workshop, with Mary, the virgin mother. A peaceful and hidden life as a manual worker in the heart of the small family circle – is that the answer to the question of Jesus's unknown past?

Again, neither we nor the scholars know for certain. And there are other points of ignorance. Who are those 'brothers' and 'sisters' who find occasional mention in the gospel accounts (more about this later)? And what is the precise significance of the two genealogies (Matthew and Luke)[9] that in fact supply conflicting details about the ancestors of Jesus and Joseph?

All we know for sure is that Jesus's origins, education, and early life are a closed book. One may think such questions fruitless, and yet they are valid enough. It is remarkable that somebody whose impact was so massive should also be so unknown in these perfectly ordinary biographical respects. Among those presented to us as founders of religions, Jesus alone has a personal history so impenetrably cloaked in silence.

BETWEEN CAPERNAUM AND JERUSALEM

Jesus now began to travel about Palestine urging people to believe in the good news.[10] A caravan of those days would have needed a week in which to traverse Jesus's working territory from north to south. Palestine, then, was not a large area. Galilee was in the north and contained Lake Gennesaret on whose northern bank lay Capernaum; Jesus liked to linger there, and it was from this neighbourhood that he was to attract his most fervent followers and his constant companions, the disciples, known also as apostles. Jerusalem, capital city and location of the temple, was in the mountainous south. Between Capernaum and Jerusalem, a distance of some 125 miles by foot, took place what is known to us of Jesus's life.

The gospels mention only a few place names in connection with Jesus's travels: Cana in Galilee we know of as the place where water was miraculously changed into wine; and Nain, also in the north, is recorded as the town where Jesus called a dead man back to life. Finally, there is Nazareth, Jesus's hometown (which today has approximately 40,000 inhabitants). Farther south, in Judea, Jericho is mentioned, and Ephraim, where Jesus fled in the face of threatened arrest, is mentioned once. That just about exhausts the list of identified sites. Any attempt on the basis of these meagre details to show how Jesus divided his time must inevitably fail. Only John's gospel tells us of Jesus making several journeys to Jerusalem for the purpose of celebrating religious feasts. The other three accounts limit themselves in the main to events in the Galilee area, and then mainly those that took place on the northern bank of the Lake of Gennesaret. Matthew mentions a journey farther north to Caesarea Philippi not far from the source of the Jordan.

That makes a pretty small stage for events that even today are familiar to us all from childhood – the Sermon on the Mount; the feeding of the five thousand; Jesus fasting in the desert; the crucifixion, and the post-resurrection appearances.

Many now ask if these things actually happened as we are told they did. Did Jesus really walk on the water? Did the dead really come to life? Questions such as these have been in the minds, at least of the educated, since the eighteenth century, and famous men, such as the philosopher Schleiermacher, and Dr Albert Schweitzer, have contributed significantly to the debate. Though it is by no means closed, this debate has already thrown up certain conclusions that few scholars are now inclined to doubt. The point is that the four gospels, which together constitute the primary testimony concerning the life of Jesus, cannot be regarded at all points as reliable and factual reports. In their pursuit of the historical truth, scholars nowadays use some fairly exhaustive and critical methods of textual analysis. One of their objectives is to determine with an acceptable degree of probability which of the sayings attributed to Jesus[11] he actually uttered, so as to distinguish these from other sayings whose authenticity is doubtful and which indeed are quite possibly the work of the gospel writers. So far no one has been able to construct what might be called a reliable basic gospel. Neither is there agreement about the authenticity of the miracle accounts. What we know for sure is that Jesus travelled about the country preaching the 'good news' (*euangelion*) of the coming 'kingdom of God', and he may while doing this have assisted some people who were ill or spiritually uneasy.

But what is amazing is that this activity that took up somewhere around two years was sufficient in impact and duration to set in motion what we now know as Christianity. The philosopher Karl Jaspers put forward four 'paradigmatic personalities': Socrates, Buddha, Confucius, and Jesus. The range and depth of their historical impact is beyond compare.

Other writers have described Jesus as the founder of a religion.[12] They see him as one to whom can be traced the start of a world religion, just as Islam began with Mohammed, or Buddhism with Buddha.

But no matter who Jesus is compared with, or from what point of view the comparison is made, the fact remains that no other religious or philosophical figure spread his teachings in so short a time, and none died as young.

JESUS'S MISTAKE

Jesus's preaching and actions all proceed from the supposition that, as he put it, there are 'some standing here who will not taste death before they see the Son of man coming in his kingdom'.[13] The Son of man and his coming – on the clouds of heaven, as Jesus puts it elsewhere – will coincide with the end of the world. And that was said to be imminent.

Jesus limited his preaching to Israel, and at first the apostles themselves never thought of extending it elsewhere. Christianity's first decades were full of the notion of the approaching end of the world. Only very slowly did more sobering thoughts enter in. The bridegroom was in no hurry.[14]

There is no historical evidence that Jesus had in mind a mission that would embrace all peoples, so conclude the experts, and any passages in the gospels that suggest otherwise were placed in Jesus's mouth retrospectively. Not a few exegetes have assumed that Jesus experienced his most bitter disappointment as he lay dying. Until the last, they suggest, he was expecting the end of the world and the final judgment. Others are of the opinion that once he had clearly perceived the inevitability of his own death at the hands of the authorities Jesus had satisfied himself with a sort of

s death and the end of the world.
me, the judgment was, as it were,
it hope of the kingdom, of the
Jesus had called his teaching the
or those who did not refuse the call

sus's expectation of the imminent end
ing of something wholly different was
with his teachings that his enduring
continuance as before, must seem very

d not end, the fundamental idea retains
ic concern, namely his insistence that a
cause death comes inevitably to all men,
act that it was not displaced by his error.
Jesus's indestru___ y undoubtedly has much to do with the
nature of his death. 'Whether we like it or not, Jesus remains as an
individual, suffering and dying.'[16] For this altogether Jewish
experience of suffering, the contemptuous comment of his
opponents who implied that his claims were illusory – 'If you are
the Son of God, come down from the cross'[17] – is irrelevant.

THREE FACTS

Whoever, like Jesus, lives in the expectation of an imminent end of
the world attaches small importance to the social order. At this
point, we come to the question that lies at the heart of this book:
What was Jesus's attitude to the society in which he lived?

The answer to this question is determined in the first place by
the event in Jesus's life that ended it, and that is historically most
reliably attested – his execution.

Of the historical figures comparable with Jesus, only Socrates
(d. 399 BC) suffered a similar end: he was accused of godlessness
and of corrupting youth, and so was condemned to death. In his
case, he voluntarily drank the hemlock cup.

But unlike Socrates, Jesus died young and, given the brief
duration of his effective ministry, the anguish of his death has

15

something very violent about it. Whereas the opponents of Socrates in Athens had had many years in which to forge their dislike of him into a desire to see him dead, the scandalous nature of Jesus's attitudes and behaviour led a great deal quicker to the final catastrophe.

In Jesus's case, therefore, the speed with which everything happened brought more vividly to light than was the case with Socrates the strong contrast between his own position and that of society at large, or at least that of its representatives. It was a contrast that was judged and punished as criminal and the execution took place outside the city, in accordance with custom, thus indicating that the delinquent had placed himself outside the accepted order of things. The mere fact of Jesus's execution is sufficient to mark him clearly as a social outsider.

This sociological conclusion is supported by two further historical facts that have their roots in Jesus's life and whose influence on the development of Jesus's fate are clearly recognizable. There is the fact of the insignificance of Jesus's own clan when it came to a regulation of the leadership question within the religious move-ment that gathered momentum after his death, and the fact that Christianity first spread itself in the lower social classes of the then Mediterranean world.

In each case an exterior element also emerges. For neglect of kinship was – and is in part today also – something most unusual in the Near East. Mohammed died without male issue but Abu Bakr, the man who claimed the right of immediate succession, was one of his fathers-in-law. And in all the succession struggles of Islam – the so-called Caliphate question – the decisive factor was that of membership of Mohammed's own clan. There were undoubtedly similar situations in very early Christianity (more about this later) but the point is that Jesus's clan could make no headway. Even in the development of a priestly caste within the young Christian communities, a development that Jesus could never have endorsed, the absence of family sentiment established itself clearly as a new feature within the history of religion. The Christian Church of the first few centuries was the first in history to know a priestly caste that did not depend for continuity on the heredity principle. For up to that time the priesthood in all known cultures was something inherited within certain selected families. But the triumph of Christianity within the Roman Empire put an end to all that.

Jesus preferred to look among the less privileged classes of society – the poor and the socially ostracized – for the conditions in which such attitudes as indifference to money, property, or social status might flourish. Paul collected money for the Christians in Jerusalem: they were poor. Around AD 180 a certain Celsus poured scorn upon the stupid preachers of Christianity who looked more like itinerant labourers than scholarly teachers. From the very beginning, care for the poor, the orphaned, and the sick was an important concern in the life of the Christian communities. It appears that there was no lack of needy people among them. This original propagation of Christian teaching among the poor is evidence of the enduring effect of impulses contrary to the social stratification and presuppositions of those times.

These three historical facts – criminality, independence of family, and the tendency to spread downwards – are central to the argument of this book, which is about Jesus's own social attitudes. But ultimately we shall get nowhere if we are content merely to separate out historical fact. When talking about outsiders we are concerned potentially as much with the rebel as with the harmless fool and the crank, with the genius as much as with the criminal, so what sort of outsider Jesus was remains to be determined. But first we shall discover in what sense Jesus was an outsider, and this we can do on the basis of the gospel texts.

WHICH JESUS?

This is the question[18] that concludes a recent study of the current position of scholarly and confessional debate about Jesus. The question is justified, for scholars have developed various pictures of Jesus, and the popular conceptions of him are certainly no less varied. So numerous are they that to enumerate and classify them would be tedious. Instead, we can restrict ourselves to an account of the conceptions of Jesus that dominated in the first few centuries.

Jesus in bad company

To begin with, there is the Jesus who was born a few years before Christ and who was crucified about AD 30. This is the man whom the biblical scholars (also called 'exegetes') call the historical Jesus. Of this Jesus little more can be said, except perhaps in relation to his teachings, than I have said already. The historical Jesus results from a critical examination of all available sources, principally the gospels, an examination that has been going on since the seventeenth century. He is a product of scholarly research. What he was really like and what he actually taught and aimed at, we can know of only indirectly and in outline.

Better known than the historical Jesus is the Jesus of the gospels and the other New Testament writings, all of which date between AD 50 and 100, and which are available in every bookshop. Each New Testament writer has a somewhat different way of presenting his subject so that Jesus comes to us in varying guises. In John's gospel – a relatively late document – for example, Jesus is God writ large: 'Before Abraham was, I am.'[19] In the so-called Letter to the Hebrews, Jesus's crucifixion attains cosmic significance; the Saviour is presented as the only legitimate high priest whose sacrificial death reconciles God and man. In the gospels of Matthew, Mark, and Luke – known collectively as the synoptic gospels because these three writers wrote from similar points of view – Jesus emerges in more human terms. But the central point is always the Saviour's miraculous resurrection, and Jesus is addressed by the aristocratic title of 'Lord'. However piously the New Testament texts were put together, biblical scholars remain mistrustful concerning the historicity of what is reported. The Jesus that emerges they call the Christ of the Bible, or of faith, a figure that should not be equated with the historical Jesus.

The third level at which Jesus may be examined is at that of the Christ of dogma. Debate about Jesus, enthroned at the right hand of the Father, is evident in the Acts of the first ecumenical councils, such as that of Chalcedon (AD 451, today Kadikoy, opposite Istanbul): in Jesus Christ there are two natures, unmixed and unseparated, the divine and the human, united in one person.

What the history of dogma contains is not something that Jesus himself put forward. This well-attested fact led the Danish philosopher and theologian Søren Kierkegaard to conclude: 'Faith is indifferent to historically attested data about Jesus; to faith it matters only that God was in the world and was crucified.'[20]

Such an argument is a result of theological concern and a theological approach and as such has no place in this particular book, whether in an explicitly confessional form or otherwise.

It is more difficult to distinguish between the historical Jesus and the Christ of the Bible, or to put it differently, between those gospel texts that in all probability are to be attributed to the historical Jesus, and those that should be laid at the feet of their pious authors, or perhaps result from the pious interpretations of Jesus current among the first Christians. Modern exegetes question the authenticity of every single word attributed to Jesus, and unanimity on any particular point is rare: what the one considers to be indisputably a true saying of Jesus is argued by the other to be the product of an over-enthusiastic editor.

With these sorts of arguments going on, it can easily happen that nothing constructive emerges at all but instead some spare and meaningless formulas of interest to none. In the process, Jesus will have vanished somewhere behind the apparatus of scholarship.

But where the highly specialized exegetical disciplines founder, the sociological approach may prove more useful. For the argument of this book concerning Jesus as outsider can rest upon data – the three historical facts mentioned earlier (page 17) – whose historical authenticity is beyond dispute. Whatever material we draw upon in the course of developing our thoughts about the gospel texts, and for the purpose of clarification and illustration, can therefore the more readily be introduced without prejudice. It may be found that one piece of evidence or another put forward by the textual critics does not hold water; this need not affect the central argument.

This argument can be developed at various levels. In the following two chapters I shall discuss the notion of deviant behaviour in connection with Jesus; I shall also attempt to explain the fact that in the eyes of Christians nowadays Jesus is not really seen as an outsider figure. The rest of the book will consist of an examination of Jesus's attitude to the major social realities of his time: religious and family institutions, social stratification, and the apparatus of economic and political power. Finally, I shall attempt an analysis of the group that first attached itself to Jesus.

In the concluding chapters I shall consider the outsider element in Jesus as the starting-point for a possible attitude to life appropriate to modern times and conditions. We shall come across Jesus in doubtful company – among heretics, innovators, and fanatics, fugitives from the world and revolutionaries, neurotics and fools, hysterics, mystics and saints.

That talk of this sort is rarely heard from the pulpit is well known, and that perhaps is one of the reasons why there sit beneath the pulpit so few people who come, or search, for more than simply consolation, more than reassurance about the comforts of an afterlife, with perhaps a little bit of moral reproof thrown in. It is this 'more' that this book is really about, even if there is no mention of it in so many words.

Chapter 2
Criminal behaviour

Whole libraries have been written in answer to the question of precisely why Jesus was executed, and much careful thought has been given to the conduct of his trial. It has even been said that Jesus died owing to a misunderstanding: Jesus suffered the death of a political criminal because his influence and objectives were thought, wrongly, to be of a political nature. And it is quite true that in the passion accounts, set out in such detail in each of the four gospels, quite a variety of accusers is brought forward: high priest, the Sanhedrin, Pontius Pilate, and a shouting mob. And in Herod a puppet king as well. Their cumulative effect is to bring Jesus down. At the end, a text was fixed to the cross: 'Jesus of Nazareth, the King of the Jews'. Disappointed Messiah expectations, political uprising, blasphemy, plain, straightforward rebellion, even a *coup* – all these have been put forward as possible causes leading to Jesus's execution. The historically authenticated aspects of it all are the night-time arrest, Pilate's verdict, the journey to the place of execution, and the crucifixion itself. But there is also the all-important fact – decisive for our present purposes – quoted by Luke from Isaiah, that Jesus was 'reckoned with transgressors'.[1] The Greek version uses a more specific word, *anomos* (illegal; malefactor, evil-doer), which we nowadays would translate by the word 'criminal'.

According to Luke, Jesus was held to be a criminal and so was treated as such. But the Bible defends Jesus against his persecutors: He was 'as a sheep led to the slaughter'.[2]

The Bible also states the causes of this injustice against Jesus: culpable wickedness or ignorance. Peter put forward the latter cause in an address to the people: 'And now, brethren, I know that you acted in ignorance, as did also your rulers.'[3] The first cause is recognizable in the curse the Jews laid upon themselves, as quoted in Matthew: 'His blood be on us and on our children.'[4]

The fact that Christendom opted for wickedness as an explanation for Jesus's death has cost many Jews their lives although, but also perhaps because, the explanation is worthless. But also the milder explanation for the guiltless execution of Jesus – the assumption of ignorance on the part of society concerning Jesus's true intentions – can hardly satisfy objective interest in what actually happened. In fact it would be quite as unsatisfactory as the explanation that bases the entire process on a misunderstanding. With a little patience, even fatal misunderstandings can be clarified, even if, as in this case, somewhat late in the day. But this would make Jesus into a perfectly harmless man to whom something unpleasant happened through no fault of his own. The explanation could then be replaced by some frivolous turn of phrase, such as that an unfortunate chain reaction of events led to Jesus's execution. But this does not deal satisfactorily with the debate – a debate that for the Jews themselves, to repeat the point, has been a dangerous one; the recurring questions are merely quietened, and that is not enough.

JESUS AS CRIMINAL

Sociologically, the position is that through the agency of its leaders a certain society (namely, that of the Jews around AD 30) saddled one of its members (namely Jesus) with heavy sanctions. In considering these points we should not forget that the major political influence at that time came from Rome, whose interests by no means coincided with those of the Jews.

In Jesus's case, both political systems – the Jews through the Sanhedrin, and the Romans through Pilate, the resident governor – worked as one, although the precise circumstances are not at all clear. What probably happened was that the Sanhedrin delivered Jesus to Pilate who in turn imposed the death penalty. In any event, both these authorities judged Jesus's behaviour to have been criminal. But what did they mean by 'criminal'?

Like all deviant behaviour, criminal acts are defined as violations of those precepts that society has issued. Such legitimate expectations find their strongest expression in the requirements of the law operating at the time, requirements that may exist in the form of sacred tradition – as in the unwritten cultures – or in literate societies in the form of written law. Whoever, therefore, contravenes such legal norms is marked as a criminal and is subject to punishment in the manner prescribed by the society concerned.

From the strictly sociological viewpoint, criminality is not a pejorative term but a word for a particular form of behaviour. There are circumstances in which criminal behaviour is normal – for example the use of drugs among young coloured people in certain American slums: in a milieu such as this one who has never tried a drug of some sort is regarded as an outsider and is despised by his peers. We also know that behaviour judged criminal by one society may be considered praiseworthy by another. There is no such thing as criminal behaviour pure and simple.

This means that the question of criminal behaviour in Jesus's case can be answered objectively only in terms of the legal norms that operated in the society in which he lived. In as far as he violated them he behaved criminally, and if he did not offend against the law then his condemnation is the result of a despotic act, or of the misunderstanding mentioned earlier, or we are concerned with a miscarriage of justice.

But a miscarriage of justice seems very unlikely. Though it is within the bounds of possibility that Jesus had become the innocent victim of political intrigue, the openness of his own behaviour, and especially his voluntary progress to Jerusalem – in itself not unlike a demonstration, as though he wanted to provoke a definite response – would appear to contradict such an explanation.

One cannot reject out of hand the possibility that Pilate's condemnation of Jesus was wholly arbitrary. We know from quite independent, non-Christian sources that Pilate had a reputation for harshness, and it would be in character for him to make quick work of an irritating and possibly dangerous fanatic. Be that as it may, the fact remains that Jesus only became involved with Pilate because the Jewish authorities delivered him up to the Roman governor, and our knowledge of the formal workings of Jewish society precludes the possibility that this action was taken without what they would have considered good cause.

Thus we are obliged to take as the most likely cause for the confrontation the way in which in the course of his public life Jesus disregarded Jewish law, claiming for himself the authority of God.

We may conclude that, judged by the norms of the society in which he lived, Jesus's behaviour was criminal. Pilate, then, was brought in to resolve the conflict between Jesus and society.

To declare a society – in this case Jewish society at the time of Christ – morally guilty because it took steps to defend its way of life against a particular individual – in this case Jesus – seems today to be somewhat invidious. All the same, one can see why this is precisely what the Christians did. Gradually, in the West, a social code became established that in many respects contradicted that of the Jews so that what began as a charge made against them in the Christian sub-cultures of the early Church became later a law against the Jewish minority in Europe. Jesus – by this time no longer Jesus but God himself – inevitably became in this situation the innocent victim of a callous people – exactly what the evangelists had already said he was. But historically and sociologically that is not how things look: Jesus's behaviour was criminal, and he was punished accordingly.

HE IS BESIDE HIMSELF

Even in his lifetime Jesus was a controversial figure. A lot of people seem to have believed him to be a reincarnation of the prophet Elijah, whereas others acclaimed him as the long-awaited Messiah. But yet another theory was put forward: we are told in John's gospel that some thought him mad.[5]

In Mark's gospel we learn that, because of the uproar he was causing, his relatives were prepared to take charge of him. They said: 'He is beside himself.' And indeed, one is strongly tempted to explain Jesus's outsider position by arguing that his mind was disturbed; at least a mild neurosis, one might argue, would go some way towards explaining his unusual behaviour. In modern societies, socially maladjusted people are frequently found among the young and the old, and we are told that those with poor adaptability have negative attitudes, and show dissatisfaction, dejection, and an introspective attitude that is remote from reality.

Try hard enough and you will find most of these characteristics in Jesus. In any event, not even with the best will in the world could he be declared a socially well-adjusted person, for as was pointed out earlier he brought society as he found it into question by declaring his early expectation of the end of the world.

With that, however, not much is said from the psychological viewpoint, or even from the psychiatric. For to construct an image of Jesus's personality that modern experts could consider reliable we would need certain data which is, unfortunately, denied us, such as details of his physical characteristics, his family status, the factors that influenced him, and so on. Neither can we subject him to any of the usual tests, nor draw conclusions concerning his personality on the basis of our knowledge of what he said and did – at least not if precise criteria are used. We have already seen that for such purposes the biblical material is far too fragmentary and unreliable in its detail. In this situation, speculation about, for instance, the relationship between genius and madness would seem to be unproductive and so will not be attempted.

To sum up: there will be no attempt in this book to produce a psychological reconstruction of Jesus's personality. The outsider element in his behaviour will have to remain unexplained in psychological or psychiatric terms. Neither is it particularly plausible to assume that Jesus suffered from some serious mental illness. In the first place, and speaking strictly, there is no *a priori* conclusive connection between the outsider role and mentally abnormal or pathological behaviour. It is therefore not necessary to attempt to adduce any such connection, which in this case means that we are not required to argue from Jesus's outsider position to a disturbed mind. Besides, given Jesus's influence on posterity – consider the category of 'paradigmatic personalities' mentioned earlier – the madness hypothesis seems extremely improbable. To put it more directly, so far no madman has ever exerted an influence comparable with or as enduring as that of Jesus, or with that of the historical personalities one might compare with him.

We may conclude that it is most improbable that Jesus's mind was in any way 'disturbed' in the clinical sense of the term. But the fact that some of his contemporaries took him for a fool is nevertheless significant. Apparently, in the eyes of these people Jesus's behaviour was so markedly irregular, so little, to use sociological jargon, in accord with the institutionalized behaviour expectations of his day, that many of these contemporaries resorted to the solution still applied today when an individual or a group behaves abnormally: they called him a fool and felt satisfied that in doing so they were setting the world right once more.

EATING AND DRINKING

In one respect, namely that of eating and drinking, Jesus's behaviour seems to have been unremarkable. Often in the gospel accounts he is seen as a guest at table, and he seems not to have shown any ascetic tendencies. At one meal there appears to have been a real scandal. A woman, who for reasons not presented in any detail seems to have been of bad reputation, kissed Jesus's feet and bathed them in perfumed oil without his remonstrating with her in any way. On the contrary, he defended the woman's unconventional behaviour: 'Your faith has saved you; go in peace.'[6] There is none of the obstinacy of the ascetic in this story and its absence seems to have influenced the disciples. Jesus told them to eat and drink what was put before them.[7]

But precisely by adapting himself to the prevailing conventions surrounding the process of eating and drinking, Jesus gave offence. He did so in that, seen from the sociological viewpoint, he dispensed himself from the rules governing the behaviour of his peer group.

The peer-group theory alleges that the individual person acts not only in accordance with the behaviour patterns generally valid in his society, but that additionally he lives by certain standards that have particular significance for him in his way of life – for example, as doctor, teacher, or judge, but also as a citizen of a provincial town, a member of the aristocracy, or of a basketball team. The individual, therefore, associates himself not only with the generally accepted social rules, such as 'effort leads to success', but also conforms to the particular behaviour patterns of his peer group – for instance, an athlete leads a moderate life.

This spare description of the peer-group theory helps to explain what the sociologist understands by role behaviour. The individual fulfils the role assigned to him by his various reference groups. By departing from the role assigned to him he becomes an outsider in respect of the particular role expectations that he has ignored.

In Jesus's case we are able with reasonable reliability to isolate a particular peer group – though only in outline. It is that group of religious enthusiasts and ascetics that apparently existed in Palestine at that time and to which people such as John the Baptist belonged. In the understandable attempt to pigeon-hole Jesus, to place him socially, many of his own contemporaries numbered him among these ascetics – and were promptly disillusioned. They said to him: 'The disciples of John fast often and offer prayers, and so do the disciples of the Pharisees, but yours eat and drink.'[8]

One can hear in this charge what must sound very much like disappointed role expectations. Whoever, like John the Baptist, speaks of the end of the world and of the general judgment, and anyone who presents himself publicly as a preacher, let alone as a prophet, must live the life of an ascetic. The Baptist lived up to this expectation – and fed, as we are told, on honey and locusts. But nothing of that sort is heard of Jesus who, as a consequence, was accused of being a 'glutton' and a 'drunkard'.[9]

It is not improbable that before he came into the limelight Jesus moved among the ascetics, and indeed some scholars have argued that he was a member of the group known as Essenes, the group I mentioned earlier. Others believe that he was a breakaway follower of John the Baptist. There is a certain rivalry between Jesus's disciples and the Baptist's supporters discernible in the gospel accounts and this does suggest that the latter view could be the more likely.

Be that as it may, the fact remains that as soon as Jesus comes into the open he is seen not to belong to the ascetics; indeed, he is seen around in company that is socially quite unacceptable, a friend of tax gatherers and sinners.

Tax gatherers are often mentioned in connection with Jesus. He included a tax gatherer called Levi among his disciples, and this Levi immediately organized a celebratory meal[10] at which, of course, his money-gathering colleagues were well represented. On another occasion Jesus stayed the night with a tax gatherer called Zacchaeus; those who saw it grumbled and said: 'He has gone in to be the guest of a man who is a sinner.'

Tax gatherers were socially outlawed, for it was their function to collect taxes for the hated Roman occupation powers, and of course they became rich in the process. But it was precisely in such company that Jesus was to be found. Nowadays, the social equivalent of these tax gatherers would lurk somewhere in the so-called *demi-monde*; but Jesus seems to have felt at home in such dubious society, so much so that Luke is concerned to provide an explanation: 'The Son of man came to seek and to save the lost.'[11]

Whether or not Jesus himself actually used such language might be doubted. More striking is something Jesus said in response to complaints that his followers fasted too little: 'Can you make wedding guests fast while the bridegroom is with them?'[12]

The bridegroom is Jesus himself. The wedding guests are those who show trust in him. Jesus's mission is likened to a party; the fasting can start when he's no longer there.

Parties of this sort have no need for social barriers: ' "Go therefore to the thoroughfares, and invite to the marriage feast as many as you find." And those servants went out into the streets and gathered all whom they found, both bad and good; so the wedding hall was filled with guests.'[13]

If at some such feasts a guest wants to sing the 'Marseillaise', or even the 'Internationale', then let him. What matters is that Jesus never showed any signs of prejudice in his social attitudes.

Bias, or prejudice, can be considered the reverse aspect of the peer group. Precisely the predictable regularity of behaviour expectations brings with it its own (long recognized and also partially investigated) limitations, for the more closely a man identifies with his own peer group, the greater becomes his tendency to obscure the identity of those outside the group, which in turn leads to prejudice.

By not permitting himself to be lumped together with ascetics Jesus was able to associate with those whom he would otherwise have had to reject, namely people such as tax gatherers. His behaviour in this respect seems to have been remarkably impartial and it made him many enemies among those who were accustomed to thinking in terms of readily identifiable and therefore somewhat rigid social categories.

Jesus could have made things much easier for his contemporaries by presenting himself unambiguously as an ascetic. For the ascetics in those days belonged, as it were, to the establishment of social outsiders, much as clerics do nowadays. Just as it is not seldom expected of a cleric that he will in some way behave differently from other men, so in those days no great excitement was caused by the bizarre behaviour of religious enthusiasts. If, for example, a man was a teetotaller and never cut his hair, then everyone who came across him knew that he was a Nazarene and took no further notice of him.

There are likely to be tolerated and as it were foreseen outsiders in most societies. Artists, for instance, are forgiven much that in other men would not be so readily accepted. An event that might otherwise be considered unusual can appear harmless simply because it occurred at the right time, in the right place, and in an appropriate setting; and anyway, the qualities of the court jester are still appreciated today.

But Jesus was no *poseur*, or wielder of gimmicks. We should not confuse his position as outsider with personal exhibitionism, as though being an outsider were simply his 'thing'; nor see in his refusal to emerge as an ascetic a particularly heightened form of snobbery. To do so would be to overlook the important fact that through his eccentric behaviour Jesus was putting his life at risk.

Jesus in bad company

In Jewish society at that time the seventh day of the week was sacrosanct. A whole range of regulations marked off the sabbath as a holy day, and these regulations derived originally from Moses and his law.

But Jesus frequently ignored sabbath requirements, as the gospels tell us. Mark reports that on one occasion a man with a 'withered' hand appeared in the synagogue on the sabbath. Jesus called the man to him and asked the scribes who were present this decisive question: 'Is it lawful on the sabbath to do good or to do harm?'[14]

Jesus's question was met with what must have been hostile silence for we are told that Jesus looked at them angrily, disturbed by 'their hardness of heart'. And without further fuss he healed the man's hand. But in the eyes of the authorities, at least, such an action was forbidden on the sabbath: 'The Pharisees went out, and immediately held counsel with the Herodians against him, how to destroy him.' This incident united two influential groups, the Pharisees and the Herodians, against Jesus. They now unanimously saw him as a criminal, and they wanted him to be punished. Jesus had placed himself above Moses and the claims he made for himself did not derive from the law of Moses. This was bad enough, but even worse was the clear implication that Jesus needed no such traditional authority for his actions. In short, he was an innovator.

The majority of those well-versed in the law were also of the opinion that in his teachings, too, Jesus had placed himself above the Torah – the Mosaic law. Matthew reports various such moments in his account of the so-called Sermon on the Mount, for example, the question of swearing oaths: 'You have heard that it was said to the men of old, "You shall not swear falsely . . ." But I say to you, Do not swear at all . . . Let what you say be simply "Yes" or "No"; anything more than this comes from evil.'[15]

The radical nature of this quite possibly authentic saying of Jesus is made the more obvious by the fact that so far Christianity has been unable to live up to it. Even today oaths are required on certain occasions, for instance in a court of law, and oaths are not infrequently sworn in front of a crucifix – the very image of him who forbade this practice.

We can see, then, that in both word and deed Jesus called the dominant norms into question, a conclusion that permits us to be more specific about Jesus's outsider role.

In 1957, Robert K. Merton, one of the fathers of the so-called structural school of sociology in America, suggested a typology,[16] well suited to the classification of outsider behaviour, that subsequently has been well received by other workers in the field. Of the five modes of individual behaviour put forward by Merton there is only one that is not typical of the outsider, namely that of conformity. The remaining four – innovation, disinterest (the jargon calls it 'retreatism'), ritualism, and rebellion – can be called modes of outsider behaviour.

That Jesus was no conformist must by now be clear enough. That his behaviour was not motivated by ritualistic considerations will be shown in the chapter following the next one. Thus, on the basis of Merton's typology we are left with a shortlist of three possible ways in which to classify Jesus's behaviour sociologically: innovation, retreatism, and finally rebellion.

Disinterest, or retreatism, is hardly something of which one could accuse Jesus. He may have told people that the world was soon to end, and this might well have led him to withdraw from all the usual concerns of life in order to prepare for the coming event. But as is well known, he did not do this; instead, and quite unequivocally, he involved himself in all that went on around him. He was never indifferent to the circumstances he observed about him; he was no stoic, and neither did he practise a doctrine of withdrawal such as that recommended, for instance, by Buddhists. And whoever, living this way, claims Jesus as his model, deceives himself. So, strange though it might seem psychologically, Jesus's doctrine of the imminently approaching end of the world did not issue in an attitude of sovereign indifference to the ordinary affairs of life.

The rebellion category seems a more promising one so long as we keep in mind his 'But I say to you' approach. Certainly there were

Thus, we must understand that Jesus's 'But I say to you' does not imply a complete break with the past; Abraham and Moses remained the acknowledged forerunners, and the God who led his people out of Egypt is also the God whom Jesus called 'Father'. Even Jesus's teaching regarding love for one's neighbour was not new in its formulation but was quoted from biblical texts.

If we cannot analyse Jesus's originality scientifically (which is not to say that it is not a fact), this does not prevent us from further reflection on this theme.

'We feel that even when all possible scientific questions have been answered, the problems of life remain completely untouched.'[19] And it is true that the problems of life are always behind man's involvement in the question of Jesus, whether the interest in him has the coolness of the scholar, the dogmatism of the know-all, or the enthusiasm of the passionate critic. So although our concern with Jesus may not spring from such impulses as motivate the collector of butterflies, we ought nevertheless and first of all to obtain a more or less dependable analysis.

It may be, therefore, that the thoughts about Jesus that I have managed to put together so far have nothing much to say to us regarding life's real problems. But at least we have reached dependable conclusions – namely, that Jesus *was* a social outsider and that this followed logically from his doctrine of renewal. The radical nature of his thought brought him into conflict with the society in which he lived and by whose standards his own behaviour was considered beyond the law: 'We have a law, and by that law he ought to die.'[20]

Chapter 3
Jesus or Christ

'And in Jesus Christ, the only-begotten Son of God' – this credal formula dates back to the second century and it is still used by many Christians today. Recent sociological investigations show to what a high extent the formula is accepted by Catholics and Protestants alike. In answer to the question whether Jesus is the Son of God a positive response of 88 per cent came from Detroit, 79 per cent from Rome, 59 per cent from Salzburg, and 42 per cent from Western Germany. The remainder of those questioned either saw in Jesus a great and important person or were unable to accept that he had ever lived.

As has already been said, Karl Jaspers counted Jesus among the four 'paradigmatic personalities' in world history (along with Socrates, Buddha, and Confucius). For Ernst Bloch, Jesus is unique in that he was wholly good.[1] Philosophers and learned men generally have tended to see and think of Jesus only as man. But some hundred and fifty years ago Hegel urged his fellowmen to consider the suffering of the incarnate God in the full truth and rigour of his God-forsakenness. For Hegel argued that religion had become inseparable from a feeling of ceaseless anguish on account of God's death – his death with Jesus on Good Friday. This ceaseless anguish, as Hegel called it, may now have changed into a certain indifference regarding the article of faith that claims divine sonship for Jesus; it is not an idea that fires people now the way it once did.

The confessional theologians, themselves bewildered by a people that cannot now be bothered even to doubt, tend to circulate their theories only among themselves. Their confusingly written books find only a small readership. In sociological terms, they – exegetes included – now constitute what has been called a 'cognitive minority',[2] which is to say that their opinions and convictions tend to be of interest only to themselves, and the question of Jesus, in the form in which they represent it, suffers a similar fate. In this situation one can well understand the longing for a Jesus more fresh than the Jesus of the clerics.

The freshness of a more candid image of Jesus is concealed beneath a layer of rubbish consisting of the ingrained habits of the believing masses who are apparently ever ready to offer worship, and who have a perpetual need to objectify their mental images, traits that are continually encouraged by churchmen. The socio-psychological processes that promote these impulses are now more or less well known, but it might be useful to set them out here even if they have no immediate connection with the object of this book.

HE WHO FOLLOWS ME

It began with Jesus's invitation to accompany him on his way. That, in any case, is what is meant by the words used in the Greek original of the relevant gospel texts. Mark says: 'If any man would come after me, let him deny himself and take up his cross and follow me.'

John's gospel has a variation on this theme: 'He who follows me will not walk in darkness, but will have the light of life.'

The process is straightforward enough, and the pattern is readily recognizable. A man approaches Jesus and asks: 'What must I do . . . ?' The answer: 'Sell what you have, and give to the poor . . . and come, follow me.'[3]

The relationship established here is that of teacher and pupil, master and disciple. The pupils accompany Jesus on his travels because they want to learn from him. Some of them are very dear to him (of this, more later); speaking for them all, Peter once said to Jesus: 'Lord, to whom shall we go?'[4] Jesus, then, is the teacher, and the disciples are his pupils. As Kierkegaard remarked, this is the Christian starting-point.[5] For those who are not contemporaries of Jesus and who yet are anxious to learn from him there is the question of being pupils 'at second hand': they cannot follow him in any literal sense as Jesus is no longer physically present·

The teacher is God; there are no pupils at second hand – so Kierkegaard vigorously affirms. 'For Faith cannot be distilled from even the nicest accuracy of detail', he argued. What matters, he concluded, is the one historical fact that God lived among us in human form. And the absurdity of such a faith would make all petty difficulties vanish and would transcend any painstaking and detailed scientific analysis (including such as is contained in this book).

In this way, faith in Jesus as God makes the scholar's approach look futile. Anyone can become a follower of Jesus just as Peter or John did. There would, then, be no material difference between Jesus's contemporaries and the believing successors of his first disciples. In essence, they are all alike. That is Kierkegaard's thesis.

But the fact that faith need not necessarily benefit thereby does not deter scholars from undertaking fresh forays into their fields of study. Attempts have been made, for instance, to trace the spiritual processes that occur in the heart of a believer as he grapples with the notion of Jesus as God. Take the case of Martin Luther, for example.

THE FIRST MASS

In a study of Luther as a young man,[6] Erik H. Erikson, a psychoanalyst of international repute, has undertaken a detailed examination of the inner struggles of this major religious intellect whose impact on the modern Church has been so significant. His findings clearly show just how decisive in Luther's development was his confrontation with Christ. The first Mass of the newly ordained monk – he was then twenty-three – was a festive occasion attended by his father, who was hardly enthusiastic about his son's chosen career. Just before the consecration the young priest was overcome by feelings of profound anxiety and would willingly have fled from the altar.[7] In those moments he had felt as though he were speaking directly to God, while behind him he could sense the worrying presence of his father. Later, Luther was to say of this occasion, as has since so often been quoted, that he 'felt no faith'. And it is

37

true that at that time he had no living concept of Christ and was torn hither and thither between the demands of obedience to his earthly and to his heavenly father. He had, as it were, overlooked something that later was to be of so much help to him and to the anchoring of his influence: the mediatorship of Christ. Five years later, as he gave his first lectures in Wittenberg, he discovered Christ within himself. But not as a stranger who died for all men, and thus as representative of all; nor as some ideal figure whom one is supposed faithfully to imitate or obsequiously to adore. The latter, to use Erikson's words, would have been no more than the surrender of a neurotic. Luther was able to see his own image in that of the crucified Christ.

'For a little while', writes Erikson, 'Luther . . . saved the Saviour from the tiaras and the ceremonies, the hierarchies and the thought-police, and put him back where he arose: in each man's soul.' Luther succeeded in curing himself of the ravages of his spiritual struggle by identifying with Jesus; in so far as Christ became the heart of the Christian identity, God lost the qualities of the earthly father whose unpredictable moods Martin had never been able to understand. God's anger had turned into mercy and it was awareness of this that enabled Luther to forgive God for being a father.

More distinct, but also more general in relevance, is Freud's account of Christ's psychological significance in *Totem and Taboo*: 'The very deed in which the son offered the greatest possible atonement to the father brought him at the same time the attainment of his wishes against the father. He himself became God, beside, or, more correctly, in place of, the father. A son-religion displaced the father-religion. As a sign of the substitution the ancient totem meal was revived in the form of communion, in which the company of brothers consumed the flesh and blood of the son – no longer the father – obtained sanctity thereby and identified themselves with him.'[8]

In psychoanalytical terms, identification with Christ is capable of counteracting the despotic arbitrariness of the heavenly father. In Luther's case this internal process had a healing effect and, according to Erikson, pushed Christian ideology a significant step forward. At this point in our discussion we have to face the question of why it was that by resolving the question of Christ's meaning for him Luther was able to achieve something that had eluded Christendom for the preceding 1500 years. In raising this question we come up against a mass-psychological process that started early on and that led to the development of that very form of the Church against which Luther was finally to revolt.

DEIFICATION

Although Paul, Jesus's missionary, was not to achieve anything like an overnight success for his doctrine of the crucified Saviour – 'a stumbling block to Jews and folly to Gentiles'[9] – by the time the period of Christian persecution was over some ten per cent of the Roman Empire's population was Christian.[10] Another 150 years later Christians constituted a significant majority and had begun to establish themselves among those peoples, the Teutons and the Slavs, who were soon to inherit the Roman mantle.

Within 500 years all that was achieved. But Christianity was not the only religion to spread so successfully. Islam and Buddhism developed a similarly powerful influence in cultures that differed from their parent culture – as, for example, Buddhism in South-East Asia and China, or Islam in Persia and North Africa. Arnold Toynbee saw a connection between this phenomenon and the decline of the universal states that had preceded the birth of the world religions in question,[11] a theory that while it doubtless rests on historical fact should also alert us to the mistake of seeing in the succession of two events a causal connection: as logic tells us, such a connection does not necessarily follow.

However, we are justified in observing in the similarity of the history of the diffusion of the great religions a law to which all three religions were subject. This conclusion was reached by Max Scheler (d. 1928).

'The most consequential – and exclusively sociologically conditioned – process in the history of these religions – the process that alone makes possible the formation of a Church and the claim of that Church to absolute authority in matters concerning salvation – seems to be always the same wherever such organizations arise: the deification, variously formulated, of the founder' (Scheler).[12] Scheler argued that initially Buddha and Jesus were models with whom their followers strove to identify, figures whose precepts one obeyed and whose teachings one believed.

But almost at once a process set in that turned these figures into cultically venerated objects of devotion by attributing to them divine origins. In Jesus's case, this process began with Paul as the cult of the glorified Christ, and came to fruition in John's gospel (written at the end of the first century). John presented Jesus as light and life, as the Son of God pure and simple.

Scheler went on to argue that the deification process had a two-fold effect, particularly as regards the great mass of the faithful. On the one hand the founder becomes an absolute authority by virtue of the unique relationship with the godhead attributed to him by his followers, thus binding the latter to him through a highly developed sense of group identity and consequent feelings of solidarity. On the other hand a process of exoneration is involved. The deification process absolves the community from the severe demands of following in the founder's footsteps, for how is a mere mortal to measure up to a being who by definition is either God himself or at least of divine origin? Thus deification brings with it alienation from the founder: as the God out there he can be offered worship but not seriously imitated.

In Scheler's view, the success of the great religions lay precisely in this deification process. It made it possible to gather adherents to the new faith without it being necessary to require from them the uncompromising attitudes of the initial few. History would seem to confirm Scheler's opinion in this respect, for in all the great religions it has so far been only a relatively small inner group or circle that has ever attempted to live by the strenuous demands of the founder to the neglect of other interests. 'Their function is to confront the enemy who call themselves Christians, but who cannot live as such, with the recurring presence of those who truly do.'[13] For the weak – back now to Scheler – we have those institutes of mass salvation, the Churches. These exist as a consequence of the basic process, namely the deification of the founder.

As soon as the original process of imitation has been changed into one of adoration, the achievement of the founder becomes merely a readily available store of grace administered by the priesthood. By following certain rules that could hardly be called severe, all may share in the treasures thus put by – a glance at, for instance, the present practice of baptism as found among the major Christian Churches confirms this argument.

The deification theory presents a useful starting-point for a discussion of the causes of the transformation that Jesus underwent. It was deification that hindered the positive identification with Jesus that Martin Luther tried to achieve. For the more remote Jesus became, the higher his throne was placed in the heavens, the smaller grew the chances of seeing this lordly figure as an imitable reality. This transformation paved the way for what took shape in Christian medieval Europe, broke down in modern times, and is now coming to an end.

DON'T COME AGAIN

This is the command given to Jesus by the ninety-year-old Grand Inquisitor in Dostoevsky's novel *The Brothers Karamazov*. The command features in the now famous encounter in this novel between the prince of the Church and Jesus, visiting earth once more. Jesus himself says nothing in the course of this encounter; the representative of the Church is the only one to speak, and his monologue consists of an accusation against Jesus to the effect that for centuries he has burdened the human spirit with the affliction of his freedom, that he thought too much of man who is really much weaker and more lowly born than he realizes.

What Dostoevsky here uniquely achieves in literary form is confirmed by history – in this case the history of anti-Semitism on the part of Christians from St John Chrysostom (d. 407), through Luther, and up to Adolf Hitler. From the socio-psychological viewpoint the deification theory is confirmed by the hatred shown by Christians for Jews: both, that is the deification and the anti-Semitism, spring from one and the same primary cause – the suppressed desire to rebel against Jesus and his claims.

Here is a quotation from a book on social psychology: "The attack against the Jews, who are accused of deicide, serves the anti-Semite as a form of protection against his awareness of his own desire to rebel against all the qualifications that have been placed on Christian morality. The anti-Semite achieves this by transferring to the Jews his own wish to destroy Jesus. Psychoanalytical theory calls this projection – one of the major defence mechanisms of the ego against demands made on it by both the id and the super-ego.'[14]

The Christian's feeling of aggression towards Jesus, who demands the impossible of him, is satisfied by the creation through projection of an external enemy – in this case, the Jews. One is better equipped to cope with external enemies than with interior ones – so the Jews are burned and Jesus remains unmolested. But even more is achieved: Christians as a group are enabled through this projection process to forget their feelings of aggression towards Jesus.

It says a lot for Dostoevsky's genius that he was able to drag this enmity towards Jesus into the light of day and to demonstrate its existence through the words of a cardinal. Dostoevsky's treatment of the situation also enables us to understand the Grand Inquisitor's statement that 'we shall be forced to lie'.

The fatal century as far as the Jews are concerned was the fourth. It was in this century that the first ecumenical councils were held, and one of their actions was to formulate the fundamental dogmas of the divine sonship of Jesus. The connection between deification and anti-Semitism is not only socio-psychologically explicable but is also identifiable historically.

Deification, therefore, is a process in which the mass of believers subject themselves totally to the glorified Christ but, as we have seen, without identifying with him. Any remaining feelings of aggression towards this deified figure are transferred to the Jews. In this process Jesus the man, the Jew, is pushed out of mind, forgotten, although, as we shall see, without complete success.

Through deification and anti-Semitism Christendom has largely disburdened itself of the task of following Jesus and in collective terms it has done this effectively. Proof of this is to be seen in the

Christ the King figures enthroned in the apses of ancient churches.

But this is not to deny that belief is still expressed in Christ's eventual return, at least in formal terms, though no one much looks forward to it, for when he comes again he will come to judge, and to separate the sheep from the goats. Who can say now on what side he will then stand? In this anxiety lies the collective punishment for what was collectively ignored, namely, the question of the real Jesus. And mixed in with this fear of Jesus as the judge is the wish that he will not come again, but will stay just where he is.

TRULY MAN

What I have just described is the state of mind in which for a thousand years many people have lived in Christian Europe. It is not easy to admire their moral stance, at least not since Auschwitz and the like, in spite of their Gothic cathedrals. These buildings represent the impressive compactness of a world picture in which Jesus had become the lord of creation. From his heavenly throne the Christ-God rules over all things. Men lived in small, miserable houses of wood and clay and erected churches that towered majestically into the sky. Even the palaces of pope and emperor, themselves symbols of the divine power, looked insignificant beside the cathedrals. The people dressed in coarse materials, and even for many of the gentry a warm winter garment that at night could double up as a covering against the cold was a barely achievable luxury. But for bishop, priest, and deacon, as also for emperor and monarch, the finest materials and the most varied wardrobes were available as they performed the manifold services of the King of kings.

This King of kings was Jesus – with the Holy Spirit in the glory of God the Father. Thus sang the choir during High Mass, and the people saw it that way too when they carried his cross. Even Jesus in the form of the host was adored rather than eaten, though the host is nothing if it is not food; preserved in lavishly ornamented tabernacles, or housed in a golden monstrance amidst clouds of incense, Jesus, even as the holy bread, was pushed into the background.

43

Remote though he was on his heavenly throne, Christ the King participated nonetheless in earthly power, for it was he who crowned the emperor and thus legitimized his reign. About the year 1050 Henry III had a dedicatory picture painted for a copy of the gospels which he presented to the church in Goslar. The picture shows the emperor and his wife receiving their crowns from an enthroned Christ. With the deification of its founder, the Western Christian Church became the most significant force in the political world, inseparable from it even in dispute. Throne and altar supported one another and the way of thinking that made this seem right and proper persisted until late into modern times. Through a reversal of his historically attested outsider position, Jesus had become the guarantor of temporal dominion. His position on the supra-temporal throne incorporated in calm immobility the fundamental principle of socially and politically effective power – stability.

Jesus himself, astonishingly, offered stubborn resistance to this type of aggrandizement. The stable at the beginning and the cross at the end, no matter how one looks at them, hardly suit the subsequent figure of a Christ-King. But thanks to the Bible, which though tendentiously interpreted could not be forgotten, memory of the real Jesus was never entirely lost. 'No matter how much it was interiorized and spiritualized, the imitation of Christ remained primarily an historical and only then a metaphysical experience. The real nature of Christ mattered greatly to those who believed in him, giving them, in anaesthetizing sameness, what no purely cultic or otherworldly image could ever have provided.'[15]

Christ as the man of sorrows achieved fresh prominence in the Late Middle Ages. The crusades brought familiarity with the land in which the real Jesus had lived. In the monasteries of the newly established orders the monks and nuns contemplated Jesus the man. 'Lord Christ, Son of God, because of the fear which surrounded your sacred heart as you surrendered your holy limbs to suffering' – is the appeal of a twelfth-century prayer which though impregnated with an awareness of Christ as God's son is nonetheless concerned with real fear. Then pictures and statues. Jesus as the man of sorrows with the crown of thorns, the *Ecce Homo*,[16]

44

became firmly established. The image of Jesus became the image of man himself, in this case oppressed man, though as yet unrebellious. The same concepts and images explain the popularity of the stations of the Cross showing the various aspects of Christ's suffering, with soldiers in contemporary dress standing around so that no one can think that what is happening does not concern him.

An awareness of Jesus as a poor person also had a strong effect, though it was not always as gentle in its expression as with St Francis of Assisi (d. 1226). Without recognizable leaders, a type of popular movement arose in the eleventh century whose members felt that pious contemplation of the five wounds of Christ was not really enough. Observing a Jesus without property, many a sideward glance was cast at well-endowed monasteries and ecclesiastical foundations, and eventually at the hierarchical principle as a whole (on this more later). But a hierarchical Church could not tolerate such criticism. The expression 'heretic' dated from this period. Even the followers of St Francis were hard to subdue: an argument launched by the mendicant friars to the effect that neither Jesus nor his apostles possessed any goods endured into the fourteenth century, and according to its backers such poverty was the highest expression of Christian perfection. Subversive thoughts such as these spread far and fast and exerted an enduring influence.

In all this a Jesus was active who in spite of his divine nature was known to have had a human one: he was truly God and truly man. This fifth-century dogmatic formula retained at least theoretical validity among the theologians, even though they preferred to devote their attention to Jesus as Son of God. The Christ that was held up to see became with increasing emphasis the divine person.

That Jesus the man was never completely overshadowed by Christ the God is due primarily to those of whom the Church's leaders were most suspicious, the mystics and the heretics.

THE HEAVENLY BRIDEGROOM, CALENDAR GOD

No one thought of telling us what time of the year it was that Jesus's swaddling clothes were changed for the first time, and the

45

first Christians could hardly have cared, their attention being fully held by the approaching end. But that didn't prevent people later from looking for a date on which to celebrate and commemorate the divine child's birth. And so now the Christ-child comes afresh each year.

The birthday was first celebrated in Egypt in the second century, and the time was the night of 5 January. In Alexandria on this night people wished one another a happy New Year and commemorated the virgin Kore who gave birth to the God of time, Aion. Kore, the corn maiden, came from Greece and was the daughter of that country's corn goddess, Demeter, one of the most popular mother goddesses of the Mediterranean world. The next day, 6 January, was the birthday of Dionysius, the god who could turn water into wine.

Behind these strange-sounding names of gods lies a familiar feeling. The old year is dead, a new one is born, and we who have survived can make a fresh beginning. The sun will climb into the skies once more and the longest night is past.

The latter led to the choice of 25 December for the birthday of Christ. It happened in Rome where the emperor found it easier to establish his calendar reforms. These reforms included the introduction of the year of the sun (under Augustus) and the naming of 25 December as Empire Day (under Aurelian) – as feast of the unconquered sun god.

For a while, the Christians themselves had two different dates for Christ's birthday, depending on whether they lived in Gaul, North Africa, or Constantinople. Be that as it may, Jesus now had a place in the calendar and had become a part of the changing seasons with all that that implied. Though Mary was not Kore, nor Jesus Sol or Dionysius, the impulse to celebrate was a powerful one, and even today the churches are fullest at Christmas and Easter.

And Easter, too, its date long fixed by the Jewish calendar, slipped with the death and resurrection of the Lord close to the gods of vegetation, Attis, Adonis, Thammuz, Osiris, Sabazius. These were all children of the gods, of various origins, each lending the other his or her own attributes in the mixture of religions that dominated the Hellenistic Mediterranean world in which new gods suddenly rose to stardom much as pop singers do now. Death and creation were everywhere. Something would disappear in the burning heat of a southern summer, come to life again with the return of spring, enlivened through secretly administered rites in exclusive circles, finally to percolate downwards to the people.

At least a hundred years ago scholars began to detect in early Christianity certain borrowings from other religions. Take the case of the virgin birth. But in this present context something else is of even more importance. For with Jesus's reception into the cultic calendar – in addition to the deification process we have already considered – a fundamental change took place in the Christian understanding of assembly.

From what little we know of the first Christian assemblies it appears that the emotional attitude of the participant was of major importance. Enthusiasm, ecstasy, and spontaneity, found expression through the fact that many participants suddenly began haltingly to speak in tongues they had not known before, or to utter prophecies. There was no clear or even spatial separation of cultic action and discussion, prayer and conversation, and sometimes there were also loud noises.

The dominant sentiment was expressed in the words: 'Come, Lord Jesus!' 'Raise your heads, because your redemption is drawing near.'[17]

They expected total change. The form of the world will pass away, the Lord will come – and none too soon – on the clouds of heaven. The days cannot have passed peacefully for these people for the talk was all of Christ's coming, arrival and return, and the days in which they lived were literally mankind's last. Their meetings took place in an atmosphere of impatience; each day could bring the universal judgment. No room here for pious contemplation of the calendar or for the ceaseless seasonal cycle of death and rebirth, for everything was transient in any case, including nature herself and her corn–mothers and fertility gods.

And yet the seasons remained as constant as ever they had been and each passing year helped to confirm that the calendar was right after all. Expecting the end, the young women had not married, and Paul was asked what would happen in the new order of things to those who had already died.[18]

Easter was zealously commemorated every year and gradually recollection became assurance. In any event, the second century saw the descent of calm and patience, spontaneous action turned into ritual and the basis of the Christian assembly became more stable. And so it remained – until today. 'To the unbiased spectator Catholicism displays deliberation, calm, and spaciousness';[19] although its history shows that every now and again the peace was disturbed, ritual increased in strength.

Like every other cult, Christianity came up against an ancient and universally applicable law – that it should repeat its beginnings. Yet in this case the beginnings were far removed from myth, for Jesus's birth and death were historically attested. But each year they were celebrated anew and with much pomp. 'Jesus, the herald of the end, became the instigator of the sacrament.'[20]

First, the Last Supper. In historical terms it is doubtful that Jesus regarded this last and fateful meal as the beginning of a lasting cultic action. Yet in the world in which he lived this act of worship would have faintly recalled first beginnings: the altar was like a table and the priest prayed while turned towards the people. But later he turned his back on them and the meeting looked more like a frozen procession with the priest at its head. What mattered was the repetition of the beginning. At each Mass Jesus was newly present – that was what really mattered.

From the historical past emerged a present and the former events were woven into a new fabric. An example of this lies in a very old text from the office of the 6 January feast day mentioned above: 'Today the heavenly bridegroom was given in marriage to the Church because Christ washed away her sins in the Jordan. Hurrying with gifts, the wise men come to the wedding and the guests drink of the wine that was water.'

The wise men from the East, Jesus's baptism in the Jordan, and the miracle at Cana merge into one basic idea: the appearance (*epiphaneia*) of God in human form. The marriage is celebrated with him – that is the central theme – and the bride is the Church. But the notion that unites the assembled community is no longer expectation of the future, advent, but the fulfilled moment. In place of the awaited kingdom of God stands the Church.

DECLINE

The deification of the founder and the entrenchment of the form of worship, each complementary to the other, made possible the emergence of the Western conception of Church. This in turn produced its own unique creative achievements, as for instance in Gregorian music, and later in the works of composers such as Palestrina, Bach, and Beethoven. Under Charles the Great, the Holy Roman Empire came to an unhappy end and by the conclusion of the seventeenth century the collapse of the old *Catholica* into various Christian confessions was complete. Even as God, Jesus had become a prisoner of confessional disputes.

Charles V's confessor directed the dying emperor's gaze to the crucifix and told him: 'There is your security; there is no more sin; all is forgiven.'

For this, Bartolomé de Carranza was sentenced to nine years in jail; the Inquisition had smelled Lutheranism. It was no longer a glance at the crucified God that mattered but the form of words used. Piety had become toeing the line, and orthodoxy had become dogmatism. The vacuum that followed the sixteenth- and seventeenth-century wars of religion (in Germany, France, the Netherlands, and England) was filled by the propagandists of tolerance, and from that point to indifference was but a short step.

'*Ce plat roman*'[21] – for the Marquis de Sade, now once again an honoured figure, the gospels were a bore, a concatenation of platitudes. This was an attitude that had two hundred years in which successfully to achieve widespread currency and attempts to persuade people to the contrary have not got off the ground.

Today, practising Christians are a minority, and not only in Sweden or the Soviet Union. In all countries containing a majority of baptized Christians among their populations, actual believers and practisers constitute a minority and are predominantly defensive in attitude. Their social influence for the good is very small –

49

they are more closely concerned with the protection of their inheritance.

Whoever today would like to know about Jesus does not necessarily call on a priest, and if he did he could well be disappointed. The deification process is coming to an end, flowing back into history. Whether Jesus in some different guise can now enliven a tired Christianity is hardly to be predicted, though devoutly to be hoped. In any event, this book was written in this hope.

Chapter 4
I have not dwelt in a house

Here is a story from John's gospel.[1] It is midday and Jesus wants
to rest. At the time he is walking through Samaria and is halfway
between Jerusalem and Capernaum. Jesus sits down beside a well.
His disciples go into the village to buy food – perhaps it was the
village now known as Askar at the foot of Mount Ebal. A woman
approaches the well as she wants to draw some water. Jesus speaks
to her.

The woman quickly sums Jesus up: 'I perceive that you are a
prophet', she says. She asks the question that happens to be passing through her mind: Where should God be worshipped? For
between the people of Samaria and those in Jerusalem there had
for long been argument on this point. The Samaritans had built
their own temple on Mount Gerizim and were therefore in strong
competition with the temple at Jerusalem. This problem is put to
Jesus with the extra edge of local patriotism. In his answer Jesus
says that the time will come when neither the one place nor the
other will be the place for worship. God will be worshipped in the
spirit and in the truth, said Jesus, and whatever else he might have
meant by that he was clearly not referring to a building. In one
sentence Jesus removes something that for all religions, not just
Judaism, was and is of decisive importance, namely the local
presence of the Lord in temples, churches, consecrated ground,
groves, chapels, minsters, cathedrals, and religious establishments.
The religious ethos has always been most obvious where the bells
ring, and the priests live, where there are processions and where
litanies are sung, where we can light candles, baptize, marry, and
intercede for the dead. But Jesus seems to think it all unimportant;
at least if we are to judge by his statement in this story that is the

clear impression. He would put all church architects out of work, as also temple servants and all clerics, in so far as their function was a consequence of their presence in holy places, for in Jesus's view there would be no need for such places in future.

Jesus's comments on this occasion, so clearly forgotten by the Christian West, did not come out of the blue. His dislike for palaces and solid walls in general was shared by those former sons of the desert who got on very well without a temple and whose God said to David: 'I have not dwelt in a house.'[2]

NOMADIC INHERITANCE, OPEN COUNTRY

According to the Bible, the first time man offered sacrifice to his God, though admittedly in somewhat dubious circumstances, he did so out in the open. Cain and Abel each wanted to offer God a sacrifice.[3] Cain offered fruits of the harvest, whereas Abel presented the 'firstlings of his flock and ...their fat portions'. Without giving any reasons, God chose to accept only Abel's gifts, showing contempt for Cain's. Cain was a representative of the latest stage of culture, namely farming. As a protest against the favouring of his brother and what he regarded as the decision of a despot, Cain slew Abel, the shepherd. And yet the Lord said to Cain that should anyone kill him vengeance would be taken on that man sevenfold.

Cain as the bringer of civilization: but not only in so far as he represents the science of agriculture. He fathered Enoch and built the first city. His descendants introduced the blacksmith's arts, and the music of the harp and organ. Cain, therefore, though he murdered his brother, is closely associated with culture. This makes him comparable with a figure such as Prometheus, who stole fire from the gods and was punished with eternal torments. In general, one can observe that the mythical heroes and bearers of civilization are often in opposition to the supreme being, and it is significant that wicked Cain stands for what is new and that higher authorities are unable to do anything about him.

In the chapter of Genesis from which the Cain story comes God is called Yahweh in contrast with other passages from the same book in which he is named Elohim. We know today that the use of different names for the Godhead indicates (at least) two different sources that originally may well have come into being independently of one another; in any event, they were edited into one text at a later date.

In Genesis it is as though Yahweh had become quite concerned about his position as man's superior. 'Behold, the man has become like one of us, knowing good and evil.' Perhaps he will stretch out his hand to the tree of life and live for ever![4]

A similar concern can be detected in several of these ancient texts. Is it possible that a status-conscious Yahweh preferred Abel because Abel was submissive? Is Cain the sort of person who prefers to meet his God in the freedom of the open country,[5] on his own ground? One thing we can be fairly sure of is that Cain's action was one of protest.

In the stories about Abraham, Isaac, and Jacob we hear a great deal about journeys, camels, and wells where man and beast could take water, about people striking camp, setting out again and finding some other place to live. The God of these nomadic shepherd people is called Elohim, not Yahweh as later the God of Moses is known. Elohim takes an active part in the nomad's life, speaks to him in dreams, directs him here and there, tips him off when trouble is near, protects and threatens him. Altars of stone are erected to Elohim out in the open, in the manner of Cain and Abel; animals are slaughtered and the smoke rising from the offerings pacifies the angry Elohim.

Various stories are connected with the altars thus erected: Jacob spent a night in the open and in a dream saw a ladder stretching up to heaven.[6] Angels were climbing up and down the ladder. On waking, Jacob took the stone on which his head had rested during his sleep and, anointing it, set it up as a monument. In Shechem and Bethel (Bethel means 'house of Elohim') Jacob erected further altars, traditions were established, or at least legitimized, by stories built around them, and sacred places and places of pilgrimage grew up, sites vouched for by archaeological evidence and through research into the place names of modern Palestine.

This was a society that had no priestly caste: the head of the tribe was *ex officio* the priest. Their altars out in the open marked resting

53

places and recalled memories; at these altars reconciliation was established after warring tribes had fought for land or a watering hole. Elohim held the different families together for he was their common bond.

Not until the beginning of the first millennium BC, in the course of a long-lasting increase throughout Canaan-Palestine in the followers of Yahweh, was it thought necessary to have a principal sacred place for Moses's ark of the covenant. Jerusalem was chosen. According to tradition, the ark had been carried around with the people, its resting place being a tent. David (*c*. 1000 BC) wanted to build in Jerusalem a permanent resting place made of cedar wood. But he was told: 'I have not dwelt in a house.' It was Solomon (d. 931 BC) who overcame the resistance of nomadic tradition and of the God who didn't want a house anyway, and put up the first temple in Jerusalem. This was destroyed by the Babylonians in the sixth century BC and many Jews were deported into Babylonian exile. The return of these exiles under Cyrus (d. 529 BC) and Darius I (d. 485 BC), and the rebuilding of the temple, led to a considerable increase in the priestly class. Only now do we see emerging in Jerusalem that source of power that the civilizations of Mesopotamia and Egypt had already had for a long time, namely a literate priestly class with a strong political influence. And so it went on until the time of Jesus. When he was born a different temple stood in Jerusalem, a new one erected by Herod, and its dimensions made it one of the wonders of the world.

The temple, then, became Yahweh's dwelling place, there behind the curtain of the holy of holies where even the high priest could enter only once a year. One only has to think about all that to become clearer about the quite contrary implication of the Bethlehem story.[7] For according to Matthew and Luke Jesus was born there, not in Jerusalem, and first news of the birth was received by shepherds out in the open, not by priests in the temple at Jerusalem.

Luke, the more sympathetic and forthcoming of the evangelists, does tell us, however, that Jesus was taken by his parents to Jerusalem to be 'presented' there as required by Jewish law. Matthew says nothing of this: the wise men from the east got nowhere in Jerusalem and had to go on to Bethlehem. But from Jerusalem soldiers were sent out to kill Bethlehem's innocents. But the Saviour escaped. The message is clear: nothing good will come out of Jerusalem. The divine child began his life as a displaced person, an emigrant.

The stable at Bethlehem has links not with the priests and their temple religion in Jerusalem but rather with the open country of nomadic man; it reminds us of the God who wanted no roof over his head and who appeared to Moses in a thornbush, of the God who reacted strongly against the Egyptians and their pyramids and temples.

That, anyway, is the message that emerges from Matthew.

PROPHETIC ANGER AGAINST PRIESTLY STATUS

Even clearer is the existence of another tradition in the gospels with which Jesus associated himself when he called the temple a den of thieves,[8] an allusion to a passage from Isaiah written six centuries earlier. Jesus was by no means the first to criticize the temple worship. The prophets had been doing so long before him, notably such as Amos, Hosea, Isaiah, and Jeremiah, all of whom had strongly attacked the temple cult and its priestly caste.

Jesus in the temple[9] lashed out with a whip, overthrew the tables of the money-changers, scattered their money all around, and drove the merchants' sacrificial animals off the premises. The people were amazed and the high priests considered getting rid of Jesus. All four gospels report this scene but John's supplies a quotation from a psalm by way of clarification: 'Zeal for thy house will consume me.'

The reference is supposed to reduce the impact of a notorious scandal; as long as zeal for the temple still has some meaning, the whip is directed only against the corruption of something that is essentially good.

But the ancient prophets, whom Jesus so readily quotes, seem not to have been reformers. Their criticism of the temple was more radical.

Amos, the earliest prophet from among those of whom we have

written testimony, voiced the primary theme that, with variations, recurs in the so-called prophetic books of the Old Testament: I have no pleasure in your food offerings. Hosea puts things more clearly: 'For with you is my contention, O priest.' Hosea also uttered the classic formulation of prophetic temple criticism: 'For I desire steadfast love and not sacrifice, the knowledge of God, rather than burnt offerings' – sentiments that Jesus was to adopt in their most literal form.

It is still not possible to say exactly when these threats and prophecies were fixed in their written form, but it can safely be said that most of the prophetic books had been around for a few hundred years by the time Jesus was born.

The prophets' distrust of cult and ritual emerges strongly from the first chapter of Isaiah: 'What to me is the multitude of your sacrifices? says the Lord; I have had enough of burnt offerings of rams and the fat of fed beasts; I do not delight in the blood of bulls, or of lambs, or of he-goats. . . . Bring no more vain offerings; incense is an abomination to me. . . . Your new moons and your appointed feasts my soul hates; they have become a burden to me . . . even though you make many prayers, I will not listen.'

Jeremiah launched a similar attack against ritualistic religion, aiming some of his bitterest criticism against the temple in Jerusalem. He is even credited with these astounding words: 'For in the day that I brought them out of the land of Egypt, I did not speak to your fathers or command them concerning burnt offerings and sacrifices.'[10]

This statement is quite contrary to the so-called priestly writings which, as for example in Leviticus, have been preserved in moderately pure form. These writings contain clear and detailed instructions from Yahweh governing sacrificial offerings.

The priestly writings: As has already been mentioned, the priestly class became firmly established in Jerusalem between 500 and 400 BC, following the Babylonian exile. As a result of careful research, a large number of biblical passages have been attributed to a particular source and these passages are known collectively as priestly writings. Their authors or editors were priests of the temple. Their style is somewhat dry and betrays a liking for data and lists, cult being the dominant concept.

In contrast to the priestly school stands the prophetic tradition and it is in this tradition that Jesus lived and taught. His impact on the people is clear: 'A great prophet has arisen among us!'[11] As Christianity a long time ago became a matter of cult we quite naturally find it difficult to appreciate the main point in Jesus's prophetically orientated criticism of cultic worship. And yet Jesus's attitude to priesthood and temple is concerned with fundamentals and not just with superficial improvements to a situation that is otherwise acceptable.

The author of the Letter to the Hebrews did not doubt that Jesus had rendered the customary priesthood redundant: 'For it is evident that our Lord was descended from Judah, and in connection with that tribe Moses said nothing about priests.'[12] This quite clearly suggests a way of thinking among the early Christians that understood Jesus as one who had nothing to do with priests. Indeed, each of the four gospels relates how Jesus was tried and condemned by a high priest. They even record his name: Caiaphas.[13]

The same way of thought is evident in the Letter of Peter and in Revelation: 'All you who believe in Jesus are priests.'[14] Hardly an attitude that leaves room for a special priestly class, at least not in the eyes of these writers.

But what about Jesus's own statements on this subject? There is not a trace in them of any intention on his part of establishing a new priesthood. Not even the operative word – *hiereus* – is to be found anywhere in the original Greek other than where Jesus alludes to the Jewish priesthood of the time, and even then he mentions it only as a power that has to be reckoned with rather than as an important concept that would have its part in the development of a nobler future.

A priest appears in the story of the good Samaritan but he comes out of it badly, for though he sees the injured man he ignores him and continues on his way unconcerned.[15]

And that is how priests mostly appear in the New Testament: remote, and careless of a priest's true concerns. On one occasion Jesus sent a leper he had healed to a priest so that the latter could attest the former leper's return to health.[16] It was the customary thing to do. But to attempt to argue from this episode to an explicit recognition of the priesthood by Jesus is no more than a piece of ecclesiastical special pleading.

To be precise: the word priest (*hiereus*=the servant of cult) appears only eleven times within the four gospels. These were priests that Jesus took for granted, put up with, without ever evaluating their role and function in a positive way, never mind fitting them into his own view of things. Jesus's disciples are never called priests in the accepted sense; they have nothing to do with either cult or temple.

To conclude: the priesthood familiar today among the major Churches, in other words the clergy, cannot legitimize itself by appeals to Jesus for it is clear that he had something quite different in mind.

DESTROY THIS TEMPLE

It was not the Jewish people, nor the Pharisees, who brought about Jesus's execution but rather the leaders among the priests, that politically influential class of men. To them, Jesus was a thorn in the flesh. Most biblical scholars nowadays are agreed on this point though they are not yet in a position to give a satisfactory explanation of the meaning of that mysterious saying reported by Matthew and John, and one apparently that during his trial became a major point of accusation against Jesus: 'Destroy this temple, and in three days I will raise it up.'[17]

The temple building was not old, having been begun by Herod the Great in 20 BC. Most of the work was done within a decade but the finishing touches were not completed until AD 64. Six years later Titus took Jerusalem and the temple was destroyed.

Seen from the Mount of Olives it was a massive sight. On the opposite slope of the Kedron Valley enclosing walls of great height were built hundreds of metres long. Spacious squares were surrounded by generously conceived courts in the Greek style and it was in these courts that Jesus preached. There were also other courts leading into the inner sanctum. Then there were the priests' dwellings, the treasure chambers, doors of gold and of bronze, and the whole filled with colourful oriental life. It was a sight that caught the imagination of Jesus's disciples: 'What wonderful stones and what wonderful buildings!' To which Jesus somewhat drily replied: 'There will not be left here one stone upon another.'[18]

The temple upkeep was financed by taxes levied upon all male Jews over twenty. In a charming little story that Matthew tells, some tax officials approach Peter and ask if his master pays the temple levy. Peter, somewhat embarrassed, replies affirmatively. Then Jesus asks who the kings of the earth take their duty and taxes from. The answer given is from others. 'Then', says Jesus, 'the sons are free.' But rather than give offence Jesus sends Peter fishing, telling him that the required coin will be found in the mouth of the first fish he catches.[19]

Jesus the stumbling block[20] is anxious to avoid giving offence. His contempt is almost tangible it is so strong. Money is not important.

But a man called Stephen managed to offend grievously. His story is in the Acts of the Apostles,[21] and we read there that he was stoned. Stephen belonged to the Christian community in Jerusalem that was formed immediately following Jesus's death. What he said in court was subversive in the fullest sense of the word and he quoted precisely those uncomfortable passages from the prophetic writings in which the temple cult is criticized: 'The Most High does not dwell in houses made with hands . . . "Heaven is my throne, and earth my footstool. What house will you build for me, says the Lord, or what is the place of my rest?" ' The charge against Stephen was in the same terms, namely that he kept on decrying the holy places and that he had been heard to say that Jesus would destroy them.

Jesus himself once said something similar and now it is heard in the mouth of one of his followers. Stephen talked away without any apparent concern for his own fate and what he had to say does cast some light on his master's attitude to the temple. Seen from Stephen's point of view, Jesus's pilgrimages to the temple, events frequently mentioned in the gospels, do not appear to be quite such pious undertakings as at first they did. Even the gospels contain signs of what looks like scandalous behaviour on Jesus's part, and in the temple of all places, as for example when at the high point of the feast of Tabernacles he called out to the assembled worshippers: 'If any one thirst, let him come to me and drink.'[22] There are other examples, especially in John's gospel, where the temple precincts become the scene of agitation and of fierce arguments between Jesus and his opponents, where stones are taken up and angry words exchanged. Not the sort of behaviour one would expect of a pious pilgrim.

It is also worth noting that in Jesus's time there were in Palestine groups of people who rejected the dominant temple spirituality, for instance the Essenes, the ascetic brotherhood who lived by the Dead Sea and whom we mentioned earlier. The Qumran scrolls (the first of them came to light in 1947) have greatly increased our knowledge of the teachings and customs of the Essenes. We do not know for sure whether or not Jesus had any dealings with this sect but we do know that its members avoided the temple,[23] indeed, were opposed to it, even though there were priests among them.

Among the Essenes, the Apocalypses, writings quite widely known in those days, were very popular. These were visionary representations of the end of the world presented in colourful and vigorous language. There is an Apocalypse in the New Testament (it was probably written around AD 80) and in it is found a final reference to a world without a temple. Much is made of a heavenly, new future, and a metamorphosed Jerusalem, a place of which one can reasonably say: 'And I saw no temple in the city.'[24]

In all this there is a spirit of emancipation, and the prophets of old come into their own. No true temple is built of stone; the Church is built of living people. It was this sort of spirit that Jesus showed in the words that were held against him when he was brought before Caiaphas: 'Destroy this temple.' Never mind what was meant in the rest of what Jesus said – the three days in which he would rebuild the temple: the invitation to destroy it was blasphemy enough, and the anger that led Jesus to lash out at the money-changers and merchants in the temple makes things clear enough.

THE TORN CURTAIN

Some scholars argue that the prophecy of Jerusalem's destruction credited to Jesus was not in fact written until some fifty years after Christ's death, that is, after the city was sacked. Several scholars feel this way. Be that as it may, it is quite clear that with regard to the significance of the temple worship and the priestly office Jesus was at odds with prevailing opinion. For the Jews loved their temple and huge crowds gathered in Jerusalem to celebrate the major feasts, many people coming from abroad. Three of the evangelists take the trouble to make the point that when Jesus died the temple curtain was ripped from top to bottom.[25] The reference is to the curtain that separates the holy of holies, the place where Yahweh is present, from the outside world. The event is supposed to signify that God no longer lives there and that with Jesus's death the temple worship has become an illusion.

This raises the question as to whether all and any temple worship is rendered vain or only that version of it practised by the Jews.

The well-known argument put forward in Christian circles even to this day, and already evident in several New Testament passages, is that the Jews rejected, judged, and executed Jesus and that for that reason God has withdrawn from them, no longer lives among them. Their sacred texts are now called the 'Old' Testament, and the final destruction of the temple in AD 70 was the punishment meted out by a just God to a faithless people. This argument, clearly anti-Semitic, is particularly in evidence in John's gospel, and is undoubtedly an expression of the growing estrangement of early Christianity from its Jewish environment. It was an argument that made it relatively easy to justify Christian temples, churches, and other places of worship, for it led automatically to the conviction that God has now gone over to the Christians: he no longer lives in Jerusalem but is now to be found wherever Christians build their temples. In contrast, the Jews had become God-forsaken and in due course they were to discover all that that implied.

But if the truth were different, namely that Jesus and many of his followers wanted nothing to do not merely with the specifically Jewish temple worship, but with any version of it, this would give

rise to some astonishing consequences. For it would then follow
that Jewish development since the destruction of the temple in
AD 70 was in fact a realization of what Jesus had in mind: a priestless
religion.

It is a fact of history that after AD 70 the Jews had no more priests
but only the rabbi, and he was a teacher, in no way a cultic func-
tionary. This is not to say that orthodox Jews did not have their own
cultic practices, prayers, and sacred songs, and of course their
synagogues, but they never thought for one moment that God
would dwell in a synagogue or that a rabbi could serve as a mediator
between them and their God. And so it goes on today. No temple –
no priests.

But this is a situation that quite accurately reflects what Jesus
had in mind, not to mention the martyred Stephen and several of
the prophets. We are by now familiar with this concept's dominant
theme: 'I have not dwelt in a house.'

Quite a strong case can be made out for the argument that the
first Christians were indeed representatives of a way of thought
that had no place for the temple worship or for priests. The early
Christian community leaders (*presbyteroi* – the origin of our word
'priest'; and *episcopoi* – the root of the word 'bishop') possessed no
sacral functions. Their role as leaders was comparable with that of
the Jewish equivalent to be found anywhere among Jewish communities in the Mediterranean world of those days. But by the end
of the first Christian century a contrary movement among the
Christian communities was well under way. In a letter from Clem-
ent, the leader of the Christians in Rome, written in AD 96, mention
is made of a cultic hierarchy in an allusion to Jerusalem's temple
servants, the so-called Levites. Evidently the Christians were not
slow to borrow from Jewish practices, although some time was still
to elapse before the leader of the Christians in Rome was to give
himself the old name of a *pontifex maximus*, the title in former days
given to a Roman high priest. And several centuries were to pass
before the Christians started to build temples in any number, and
before the clerics attached to them began to fill the existing positions of the officially recognized priesthood. What matters is that
today this development is sufficiently well known and that it does

not accord with Jesus's views on temple worship and priesthood.

Indeed, paradoxical though it might sound, there are signs that what Jesus foresaw is more closely realized among the Jews.

If all that is true, then in this respect Jesus's outsider position is being continued precisely by a race that society has made its outsiders. While they were still around, the Jewish priests condemned Jesus. As soon as they disappeared, the Christians hastened to reintroduce them. This development, that in its turn led to the concept and reality of a 'Christian West', made the Jews quite literally into outsiders. That during this long period of suffering they showed little sympathy for Jesus the Jew is hardly surprising, for it was in his name that they were persecuted. The Jesus who wanted the demolition of the temple belongs rather to them than to the Christian Churches.

Chapter 5
Noli me tangere

In the Museo di San Marco in Florence there is a painting by Fra Angelico of Jesus dancing in a meadow in front of the empty tomb. Mary Magdalene is kneeling in front of him. The painting captures the moment of recognition[1] as told to us in John's gospel. Mary Magdalene had been looking for Jesus's body and was now weeping because 'they have taken away my Lord, and I do not know where they have laid him'.

Jesus appears but Mary takes him for the gardener. Only when he addresses her by name does she recognize him: 'Rabboni' (which means Teacher). To which Jesus replies: 'Do not hold me, for I have not yet ascended to the Father.'

Traditionally, Christian art has represented Mary Magdalene as a reformed sinner. Examine some representations of the crucifixion, particularly baroque ones, and you will have little difficulty in guessing the nature of the life she had led: even beneath the cross, when racked by grief, there is a touch of eroticism about her – the long hair, a naked shoulder.

But Fra Angelico doesn't need these visual aids. In his fresco it is clear that we are dealing with two people, a man and a woman, both wearing haloes, who have a particular friendship for one another. The intimacy of the scene cannot be doubted. The two hands are almost touching. But Jesus's gesture also suggests a discreet check – one sees that he is in fact pointing beyond Mary Magdalene. He is dancing away from her. Do not touch me: the glorified Jesus behaves on this occasion as something less than a dependable partner; the trusting woman is disappointed as, hardly found, her beloved escapes once more.

In a biblical love song, the so-called Song of Solomon, there is

64

another example of the bride seeking her lover: 'I sought him, but found him not. The watchmen found me, as they went about in the city. . . . Scarcely had I passed them, when I found him whom my soul loves. I held him, and would not let him go until I had brought him into my mother's house, and into the chamber of her that conceived me.'²

Clearly there was a happy ending – marriage, children; the world goes on, the family wins out. 'For this reason a man shall leave his father and mother and be joined to his wife, and the two shall become one' – thus the first book of the Bible as quoted, according to Mark and Matthew, by Jesus himself.³

In this, Jesus vigorously attacked divorce, which was then permitted. He argued that man and woman should stick together until parted by death, a doctrine to which the major Christian Churches have ever since been faithful. No sign here of that 'do not touch me'.

Jesus, then, is regarded as the protector of the family, and the Holy Family in their little house at Nazareth became the favourite image of a pious idyll.

But in all this much is forgotten. Jesus hangs tidily framed above the marriage bed in spite of the fact that this position doesn't suit him at all, as we shall see.

THE CARPENTER'S SON

Paul's Letter to the Romans, an old and authentic Christian text, introduces Jesus with the words: 'Who was descended from David according to the flesh.' For the early Christians to preach about Jesus to the Jews without observing that he was descended from the tribe of David was unthinkable; in those days the Messiah and the son of David were complementary concepts.

Thus Matthew and Luke provide us with the genealogies I mentioned earlier. Their purpose is clear: Jesus's role as the Messiah must be firmly anchored. Throughout the New Testament Jesus's descent from David is traced back through his legal father Joseph, of whom Luke, for example, says: 'Because he was of the house and lineage of David.'⁴

Needless to say, Jesus himself had nothing to do with these

genealogical interpretations. Until the time of his sufferings he did not emerge as the people's Messiah (on this more later), and attempts to acclaim him David's son were not gestures that he was inclined to take seriously. Historically, his origins are thoroughly obscure and he himself did nothing to cast light on the subject. On the contrary, he either ignored references to his origins or angrily rejected them.

There is a story about the scandal Jesus caused in his hometown of Nazareth when he preached in the synagogue there that contains a possible explanation. From early youth Jesus had regularly attended the synagogue services in Nazareth on the sabbath and on feast days.[5] At some point he had left the village but now, already well known as a preacher and miracle-worker, he pays his hometown a visit.

Excerpts are read from the writings of the prophets on the morning of the sabbath and every Jew has the fundamental right to take the lectern, though customarily this was done at the invitation of the leader of the synagogue. To the amazement of the community, Jesus gave a brilliant sermon. This led the people to ask how he was able to do it. ' "Is not this the carpenter's son? Is not his mother called Mary? And are not his brothers James and Joseph and Simon and Judas? And are not all his sisters with us?" . . . And they took offence at him' – that at least is the reaction recorded by Mark and Matthew, but Luke reports something like a lynch attempt. Jesus's answer is abrupt: 'A prophet is not without honour except in his own country, and in his own house.'

'In his own house.' This expression refers to the tribe and lineage. Jesus clearly expects little from them and in fact he distances himself from them.

The listing of a long sequence of ancestors when presenting someone for the first time would nowadays be considered absurd and yet to do so would accord with a pattern of behaviour widespread in pre-industrial societies. It is a question of the 'ascription' of the individual person within his society and on the basis of blood relationships. The custom also existed among so-called primitive peoples. 'The whole cosmos of the Maori unfolds itself as a gigantic "kin". . . . Apparently he does not feel quite comfortable if he cannot – preferably in much detail – give an account of his kinship. . . . With real passion the high-born Maori studies the genealogies, compares them with those of his guests, tries to find common ancestors, and unravels older and younger lines. There are examples that he has kept in order genealogies including up to 1,400 persons.'[6]

But the Maoris are not exceptional in this matter of enthusiasm about one's ancestry. No known society either now or in the past is or was without family laws of one type or another. Nowadays educational psychologists take a child's ancestors into account, sociologists concern themselves with the rules of courtship and marriage, and ethnologists and cultural anthropologists with kinship patterns. Although it is true that the question of the origins of family ties and taboos eventually becomes lost in the long and largely unknown prehistory of the human race, major thinkers – such as Freud, and more recently Claude Lévi-Strauss – have gone into the matter thoroughly and have come up with some important theories.

The universal significance of the family within community life can be attributed to a few basic functions without which society would collapse – or so our experience so far would indicate: the regulation of procreation and sexual behaviour, the education of children, economic support, social grouping according to class, and the production of a sympathetic environment. Thus, what one is and where one belongs is learnt first of all at home.

Even today a man is outwardly characterized by his family status (single, married, widowed, divorced), and descent (name and occupation of father). To consider these questions unimportant would be to be the odd man out, or such at least would be the verdict of the conforming majority, who attribute great significance to them. 'To whatever society he belongs, the individual is rarely capable of assigning a cause to this conformity: all he can say is that things have always been like this, and he does what people before him did.'[7] In this respect things have changed very little since Jesus's time.

We are told in John's gospel: 'Philip found Nathanael, and said to him, "We have found him of whom Moses in the law and also the prophets wrote, Jesus of Nazareth, the son of Joseph." [8]

What the good people of Nazareth said accords in one respect exactly with what was said by the two disciples, and from the sociological point of view is entirely predictable. Jesus's family is identified and his social origins are ascertained by alluding to his descent. In Nazareth itself the identification is more precise than elsewhere for the people there are familiar with Jesus's ancestry.

But in this respect also Jesus takes issue with the norm. One can discern a break between him and his tribe – which has little time for him. They label him a fool (as reported in another context), a fact that is as indicative of the break as Jesus's own sharp comment that comes across at its freshest in Mark's narrative: 'And his mother and his brothers came; and standing outside they sent to him and called him. And a crowd was sitting about him: and they they said to him, "Your mother and your brothers are outside, asking for you." And he replied, "Who are my mother and my brothers?" And looking around on those who sat about him, he said, "Here are my mother and my brothers! Whoever does the will of God is my brother, and sister, and mother." '[9]

This is to break the umbilical cord with a vengeance. Indeed, the apparent crudeness of the stroke leads Luke to omit in his version of the event all data that might reflect unfavourably on Jesus's family. But even Luke – and he alone – well disposed though he is to the family, does not refrain from telling a story that while clearly sympathetic to the temple nevertheless contains sure signs of emancipation.

As pious Jews, Jesus's parents would go to Jerusalem for Passover. On this occasion Jesus himself, now twelve years old, went too. On the return journey it is noticed that Jesus is no longer with them. Mary and Joseph retrace their tracks and eventually find him in the temple, 'sitting among the teachers, listening to them and asking them questions . . . And when they saw him they were astonished; and his mother said to him, "Son, why have you treated us so? Behold, your father and I have been looking for you anxiously."

'And he said to them, "How is it that you sought me? Did you

68

not know that I must be in my Father's house?" '[10]

Clearly by 'Father' Jesus means not Joseph but his father in heaven. And the way in which Jesus refers here to his heavenly father is certainly authentic, for in what he says we can discern a contrast of unmistakable originality: My father – your father. Scholars now agree almost unanimously that Jesus made a clear distinction between his personal relationship to the divine father and whatever this same God might signify for others. Jaspers called this characteristic of Jesus's personality 'the essential idea'.[11] But we should not think this means that Jesus saw himself as God; that did not happen until later, as we have seen.

But it is certain that Jesus sought and found a father who made Joseph the carpenter into an irrelevancy. There is an episode in the life of Francis of Assisi that sounds like some sort of response to this exchange of fathers. Francis is said to have gone into one of the bishop's rooms, stripped off all his clothes, and then returned naked to the presence of the bishop and his own father. There, in front of the bishop and his own father, he laid his clothes and his money on the ground and said: 'Until now I have called you, Pietro Bernardone, my father, but as I now want to serve the Lord, I am returning the money that caused the trouble and all the clothes that I ever had from you. From now on I want to be able to say Our Father who art in heaven and no longer father Pietro Bernardone.'[12]

This apparently happened on 16 April 1207. The relationship had ceased to mean anything important to Francis, descent and paternal inheritance had lost their interest, and as for marriage Francis was from then onwards to consider himself wedded to poverty as a way of life.

In this type of exegesis Jesus emerges once again in fresh and clear colours, the tribe is put in its place and even his mother is rejected, for in Luke's gospel we read how 'a woman in the crowd raised her voice and said to him, "Blessed is the womb that bore you, and the breasts that you sucked!" But he said, "Blessed rather are those who hear the word of God and keep it!" '[13]

Even in the relatively later account written by John there are two occasions on which Jesus addresses his mother with the word 'woman', which in the Semitic world of those days would have been both unusual and striking.[14]

In short, Jesus had done something in respect of his father, mother, and relations as a whole that even today happens infrequently, and in the cultural setting of his own times was quite simply unheard-of – he had emancipated himself from all family ties.

In this light it follows that not only the genealogies – including the later addition of 'son of David' – but also the question of Jesus's place of birth, are irrelevant, although it was precisely the latter question that was so enthusiastically pursued:[15] 'Some of the people said, "This is really the prophet." Others said, "This is the Christ." But some said, "Is the Christ to come from Galilee? Has not the scripture said that the Christ is descended from David, and comes from Bethlehem, the village where David was?" '

But a few people in Jerusalem knew well enough: 'Yet we know where this man comes from; and when the Christ appears, no one will know where he comes from.'

Even if these arguments in John's gospel reflect shades of debates that took place within Judeo-Christian Palestine only after Jesus's death, Jesus's own answer sounds in essence authentic: 'You know me, and you know where I come from? But I have not come of my own accord; he who sent me is true, and him you do not know. I know him, for I come from him, and he sent me.'

BETTER NOT TO MARRY AT ALL

In spite of its subversive content, what has been said so far remains in the first instance Jesus's own private affair: it is open to any man to break with his family without the action itself implying any intended public significance.

We therefore have to ask whether in Jesus's case something larger and more significant lay behind his indifference towards his own family – significant, that is, in respect of family relationships generally, marriage and procreation, including relations between the sexes.

At this point we should recall the notorious Christian neurosis with regard to sex, as in the vivid expression of it by Augustine of

Hippo, doctor of the Church and bishop, who died in 430. In his *Confessions* he writes: 'My inner self was a house divided against itself. In the heat of the fierce conflict which I had stirred up against my soul in our common abode, my heart, I turned upon Alypius. My looks betrayed the commotion in my mind as I exclaimed, "What is the matter with us? What is the meaning of this story? These men have not had our schooling, yet they stand up and storm the gates of heaven while we, for all our learning, lie here grovelling in this world of flesh and blood!" '[16]

Augustine was, of course, thinking of his mistress, who had loved him and given him a son. In the end he was to dismiss her, primarily – according to the custom of the times – so that he could marry someone of his own class. But Augustine never married: instead he turned to the Church.

Again from the *Confessions*: 'I was held back by mere trifles, the most paltry inanities, all my old attachments. They plucked at my garment of flesh and whispered, "Are you going to dismiss us? From this moment we shall never be with you again, for ever and ever. From this moment you will never again be allowed to do this thing or that, for evermore." What was it, my God, that they meant when they whispered "this thing or that"? . . . Yet, in my state of indecision, they kept me from tearing myself away, from shaking myself free of them and leaping across the barrier to the other side, where you were calling me. Habit was too strong for me when it asked, "Do you think you can live without these things?" '[17]

But the other side was already the stronger: 'But by now the voice of habit was very faint. I had turned my eyes elsewhere, and while I stood trembling at the barrier, on the other side I could see the chaste beauty of Continence in all her serene, unsullied joy, as she modestly beckoned me to cross over and to hesitate no more. She stretched out loving hands to welcome and embrace me, holding up a host of good examples to my sight. With her were countless boys and girls, great numbers of the young and people of all ages, staid widows and women still virgins in old age. . . . '[18]

Continence claimed Augustine when he was thirty-two years old. Later he was to become a bishop and as such he made it known, once again in his *Confessions*, just how troublesome to him after

fifteen years of continence was that unquenchable residue of desire:
'More and more, O Lord, you will increase your gifts in me, so
that my soul may follow me to you, freed from the concupiscence
which binds it, and rebel no more against itself. By your grace it
will no longer commit in sleep those shameful, unclean acts in-
spired by sensual images, which lead to the pollution of the body
. . . '[19] Had he been able to do so, Augustine would have dammed
even this flow of seed, and as it was, the bishop did not fail to draw
attention to his dirty linen. In the subsequent centuries, scrupulous
monks must have found comfort in this passage (Augustine's
Confessions were widely available long before the introduction of
printing).

Addressing himself to God, Augustine produced writings
whose influence lived on right into our own times: 'You commanded me not to commit fornication, and though you did not
forbid me to marry, you counselled me to take a better course.'

This refers us back to the gospels, and specifically to that somewhat gloomy passage handed down to us by Matthew: 'For there
are eunuchs who have been so from birth, and there are eunuchs
who have been made eunuchs by men, and there are eunuchs who
have made themselves eunuchs for the sake of the kingdom of
heaven. He who is able to receive this, let him receive it.'[20]

This reference to castration is the only text in the four gospels
to which Augustine and others who preached continence can
appeal – until the Council of Trent (1545–63) proclaimed virginity
a condition superior to marital status.

Let us suppose, for the sake of argument, that the text quoted
from Matthew can in fact be traced back to a saying of Jesus. It
should therefore follow that Jesus would have been at least
sympathetic to a radical form of sexual asceticism. Jesus, if anyone,
would most certainly have counted himself among those who were
eunuchs for the kingdom of heaven's sake, for as we have seen there
can be no doubt but that the kingdom of heaven was Jesus's
primary concern. Jesus would therefore have committed himself
personally to the most drastic of all anti-family stances. To marry
and be married would then indeed become an affair for the sons
of this world[21] – thus Luke – whereas in the new order of human

relationships foreseen by Jesus all family institutions, including the difference between the sexes, would disappear in the whirlpool of destruction: 'For as in those days before the flood they were eating and drinking, marrying and giving in marriage, until the day when Noah entered the ark, and they did not know until the flood came and swept them all away, so will be the coming of the Son of man.'[22]

In these sayings of Jesus, the family is clearly characterized as an aspect of a world order that is on the way out; but whoever becomes involved with such things has nothing to lose but his time.

Whether this way of thought led Jesus actually to commend voluntary castration cannot be conclusively determined, but that there were fundamental reservations in his attitude to the family as an institution is well enough attested.

For instance: 'If any one comes to me and does not hate his own father and mother and wife and children and brothers and sisters, yes, and even his own life, he cannot be my disciple.'[23]

And: 'Do you think that I have come to give peace on earth? No, I tell you, but rather division; for henceforth in one house there will be five divided, three against two and two against three; they will be divided, father against son and son against father, mother against daughter and daughter against her mother, mother-in-law against her daughter-in-law and daughter-in-law against her mother-in-law.'[24]

Further: 'He who loves father or mother more than me is not worthy of me; and he who loves son or daughter more than me is not worthy of me.'[25]

Finally, by way of summary: 'And a man's foes will be those of his own household.'[26]

From the scholar's viewpoint, it is not at all improbable that Jesus did in fact talk like this. And when, as in Matthew and Mark, Jesus is drawn into a dispute about moral questions concerning marriage,[27] he refers his partner to the degree of corruption in the prevailing customs by coming out against divorce. It is not easy, given the passages quoted above, to argue from this that Jesus was trying to protect the stability of the family. In Matthew the

73

disciples said in response to Jesus's call for marital fidelity: 'If such is the case of a man with his wife, it is not expedient to marry.'

Jesus did not contradict them.

JAMES THE LESS

On the basis of the evidence one is entitled to conclude that Jesus considered the family irrelevant to the future he projected. Following his death, those who wished to preach in his name faced a major problem: Who was to take over the leadership? Who would take the master's place when the commemorative meal was ceremonially eaten? Who would resolve disputes? Who, in a word, would be Jesus's representative until he came again?

The heart of the matter can be explained by looking at the solution to the succession problem that was worked out after the death of Mohammed (AD 632).

Unlike Jesus, Mohammed founded a religion: 'This day I have perfected your religion for you and completed my favour to you. I have chosen Islam to be your faith' – *Koran*, Chapter 5. In spite of his concubines and his four chief wives, Mohammed had no male issue and made no arrangements about who should succeed him. His closest collaborators therefore organized a vote, as a result of which Abu Bakr, one of the prophet's fathers-in-law, became caliph. Two years later, Abu Bakr was succeeded by Omar (634–44), also a father-in-law. The third caliph, Othman (644–56), was the husband of one of Mohammed's daughters. After Othman's death the clan broke up; the group led by Ali, one of the prophet's cousins and sons-in-law, was opposed by the followers of Aisha, one of the prophet's wives.

This sequence of events shows clearly that in the cultures of the Near East blood relationship was everything. The first thing to note about someone was his descent, and to this day that is the case in Arab countries. It means that an individual's first source of protection is his membership of a tribe; to break with the tribe is to invite the most serious consequences.

The same can be said of Jesus's own social environment. And indeed there is some evidence that in the first few decades following his death Jesus's immediate family was in fact involved in a vain struggle for succession.

There is no reason to doubt the historicity of Jesus's brothers and sisters or, having accepted them, to attempt to explain them away theologically.[28]

One of the family, James, also known as James the Less, quickly achieved a prominent position among the Judeo-Christians of Jerusalem. In AD 62 James was executed by being stoned to death and was followed by Simon, another of Jesus's brothers, in the leadership of the Christian community in Jerusalem. Neither of them numbered among the apostles. Nevertheless, James had the last word at the Council of Jerusalem (AD 48–9) and his resolution was carried.

In several early Christian writings this James is presented as the first among all the bishops (Pseudo-Clement) and another apocryphal text, the Gospel of St Thomas, places him above Peter.[29] Just how vigorous were the attempts of Jesus's family to involve itself in the young Church's leadership struggles cannot be historically ascertained with any degree of certainty. What is important is that they occurred and that they failed. The circle of Jesus's disciples proved the stronger and the succession question, in as far as this concerned leadership functions, was resolved through a vote rather than by family descent – which is still the case today as regards the choice of a pope.

It is true that in spite of Jesus's contrary intentions a priestly class quickly developed within the Church (as was seen in the preceding chapter), but novel in this case, as against all comparable priestly castes of the Mediterranean world, was that the role was not inherited through family descent. Such a system was ruled out from the start. Though at the outset priests and bishops were permitted to marry, no priestly élite developed that could control positions of power through family connections. This was quite the reverse of the situation common to all those societies and cultures with which the Christians came in contact, including that of the Jews (until the destruction of the temple).

The explanation for this development, whose far-reaching economic, political and cultural consequences are readily discernible, lies in the powerful continuing influence of what has been discussed as the hallmark of Jesus's attitude to the family: namely his fundamental indifference towards family ties in general.

Amazingly, this development established itself even though the expectation of the imminent end of the world came to nothing. It was a development that, in the early and late Middle Ages particularly, released considerable social forces, in spite of nepotism at the papal court. For the fact that the property of a diocese was placed securely beyond the grasp of relatives and descendants was a point of crucial importance in political and economic terms. In the unmarried bishops the Saxon emperors (919–1024) had their most reliable vassals. In the ecclesiastical hierarchy of the Middle Ages a principle became established that in all other civilizations had either not existed at all or else had done so only in rudimentary form, as for example in China: success in society as a consequence of personal achievement rather than accident of birth. The building enthusiasms of popes, bishops, and abbots even at the beginning of modern history clearly demonstrates their awareness of being without descendants. Many of these clerical builders erected their own personal monuments because the only time in which they had to do it was their time in office. The head of a noble family, on the other hand, could afford to be patient because what he was not himself able to complete his sons or grandsons would; his concern, therefore, was primarily the social position and prestige of his family.

But it cannot be denied that the principle of excluding the family was early on moderated by corruption. The sale of benefices, and nepotism, were the two chief means through which a leading family could assure itself of continuing influence in the ecclesiastical sphere. But the principle was there and it was to be protected by one reform after another, until finally the property of those unmarried men became so substantial that it provoked the emergence of fresh forces that finally destroyed it.[30] Even so, something had been relativized in this long process that in all other civilizations had been a major determining factor: the political and economic power of the leading families.

We maintain that this development can be traced back to a man whose own position with regard to the family was reserved, to say the least. That man was Jesus of Nazareth, whose dream of the Kingdom had consequences in this case that did not lie in unattainable Utopia.

THE SON OF THE VIRGIN

Exclude Catholic exegetes and you will find a wide measure of agreement among scholars nowadays about the legendary character of the accounts of the virgin birth. But to characterize these stories as legends is not thereby to deny the enormous impact and influence they have had from the socio-psychological point of view. The Swiss depth-psychologist Carl Gustav Jung (d. 1961) described in *Answer to Job* the beneficial influence the virgin mother has exerted;[31] and Erikson, a psychoanalyst and follower of Freud, considered the rejection of the Madonna following Luther's doctrines to constitute a loss for religion.[32]

Though in themselves extremely interesting, these considerations have no direct connection with the object of this book. What is important is that in the virgin birth we have a very old and extremely successful attempt to symbolize effectively Jesus's emancipation from everything to do with family – and also from sexuality. In the first place, as the son of a virgin Jesus is separated from the sexual act: his conception was an act of God. No earthly father can claim him, nor any ancestral line. And marriage of course was out of the question. As we have already seen, as a bridegroom he is reserved exclusively to the Church, as Paul emphasizes.[33] And Revelation ends with the symbol of the *Hierosgamos*, the marriage of the son to the mother-bride. But the wedding takes place in heaven where 'nothing unclean' can enter.

The effect of all this on Western culture and morality is not here at issue. What concerns us is the early onset of the Christian purity principle and its sharp antagonism to everything connected with man's sexual desire – or the 'will of the flesh',[34] as John puts it in the prologue to his gospel. Once again that still unanswered question raises its head: Is Augustine's statement that God requires continence of us in fact traceable to Jesus himself?

77

Jesus in bad company

'I came to cast fire upon the earth; and would that it were already kindled!'[35] This Jesus-saying excellently characterizes the basic spirit in which Jesus preached. And Jesus was very much in earnest; what he proclaimed was the general break-up of the circumstances in which life was carried on.

In this view of things valid ethical norms lose their claim to be absolute. In this connection it is noticeable that Jesus could be stricter even than the requirements of the Jewish Torah's moral code (for instance in the matters of divorce and adultery),[36] while on other points he gave offence by showing sympathy for sinners of both sexes. An example of the latter might be the story John tells us about Jesus and the woman taken in adultery; there we read that Jesus said: 'Neither do I condemn you.'[37]

'Jesus's ethos should not be taken as a system of prescriptions for actions in this world.'[38] Writing in the year 57 to the Christians at Corinth, Paul had to confess that 'concerning the unmarried, I have no command of the Lord'.[39]

Nevertheless, Paul offers advice and it is advice that expresses in full the early Christian asceticism: 'The unmarried man is anxious about the affairs of the Lord, how to please the Lord; but the married man is anxious about worldly affairs, how to please his wife, and his interests are divided. And the unmarried woman or girl is anxious about the affairs of the Lord, how to be holy in body and spirit; but the married woman is anxious about worldly affairs, how to please her husband.'

In saying this Paul is in no way forbidding marriage, merely devaluing it: 'The appointed time has grown very short; from now on, let those who have wives live as though they had none . . . For the form of this world is passing away.'

This sort of teaching did not go unheeded, in spite of the postponement of the world's ending. Since the Council of Elvira in Spain (c. 306) all clerics in the Western Church above the rank of deacon have been forbidden the use of a previously contracted marriage. This was the beginning of a tendency that was documented in the famous Kinsey report shortly after the Second World War: the more pious a person is – as Catholic, Protestant, or Jew – the more reserved he is sexually.[40] 'As the Christian night time came on and man found it necessary to slink towards love on tiptoe, he began to be ashamed of what he did.'[41]

The long history of sexual asceticism in Christianity need not detain us now. It leads from the first hermits in Egypt, through the long succession of ever-recurring monastic movements, up to the Puritanism of New England (USA). R. S. Lee has called this development, with its strong emphasis on chastity and obedience, a religion of the super-ego.[42]

None of this has anything much to do with Jesus.

What Jesus really thought about the family and about sex could probably be described in a sentence from what one might call the tone-setting fourth chapter of Robert Musil's novel *The Man without Qualities*: 'Well, it could probably just as easily be some other way.'[43]

In what might the difference lie? One looks in vain for an answer from Jesus. It has been sought in social forms that are now part of history but of which one might nevertheless feel that even though somewhat disfigured they contained something at least of Jesus's original attitude.

There is almost no other social institution that rests so firmly on the claim that things have always been thus. The argument did not appeal to Jesus and the attempt of his family to claim him failed.[44]

Family and sex were not able to keep a hold on him, or at least he refrained from tying himself to either of them.

Chapter 6
The downward tendency

'And Jesus, who shines as brightly as a star, will certainly not spare all those fine gentlemen', wrote François Villon (born 1431, year of death unknown) angrily, as underdog, from the viewpoint of the footpads and vagabonds, the penniless students and the questionable types who wander between the beer-house and the lock-up.[1] Here speaks a man who doesn't mince his words; no learned man need tell him that all societies have known things like class systems; or that the fine gentlemen who sit quite high up the ladder – including priests – have always tended to maintain that their position was divinely ordained, or even that it was in accordance with the natural order of things: if you're born with nothing then that's how you'll stay. Or they argue that American blacks have a lower level of intelligence than whites. There were once two brothers called Onassis. One achieved something and owned many big ships. The other became a Communist and remained poor.

Without taking up a partisan position the question of class contrasts can hardly be studied at all, for even the impartial sociologist with his tape-recorder does not relinquish the rung of the ladder appropriate to him as he comments on the fact that such class divisions exist. An income of $4000 per annum and over is preferable to one of $2000 or less. Whose bread I eat his song I sing.

The song Jesus sang to the poor was not from above where the bread was distributed. 'Jesus leaned chiefly toward the poor, the outcasts, the sinners.'[2] In short, he was partisan; came down firmly on one particular side, and it was not that of the ruling class. This tendency downwards to the poor and the despised, to the *marginales* as they are known in South America, made Jesus himself into a sort of fringe person, a marginal man.

BLESSED ARE YOU POOR

Many biblical scholars maintain that the stable at Bethlehem and the shepherds in the field are just myths. But Ernst Bloch wrote: 'People pray to a child born in a stable. And the stable can be taken as true for no one would have dreamed up so humble an origin for the founder. Legend constructs no pictures of misery and certainly none that endure a whole lifetime. The stable, the carpenter's son, the fanatic among deprived people, the gallows at the end, such data come from history, not from air.'[3]

It is a fact that the smell of poverty has never finally been blown away from the child's origins, not even by the bourgeois if liberal textual criticism of the scholars. Luke's comment has always seemed pertinent and historically reliable: 'They brought him up to Jerusalem to present him to the Lord . . . and to offer a sacrifice according to what is said in the law of the Lord, "a pair of turtle-doves, or two young pigeons".'

Only the poor made such offerings.[4]

Jesus's origins were certainly humble enough. He was descended neither from the aristocracy of the blood nor from the priestly nobility. His first followers were simple unsophisticated people, such as fishermen. A high standard of living was to be found only in the houses of kings (Matthew quotes Jesus to this effect)[5] but Jesus was not to enter such buildings until several centuries had passed; but by then he had himself been gilded.

So Jesus was not to be found in the salons nor in the schools run by those well-versed in the law and the prophets; nor was he a familiar among the ascetics of the wilderness. His first sermons were most likely, as Luke has reported them, delivered before the people: 'Blessed are you poor, for yours is the kingdom of God. Blessed are you that hunger now, for you shall be satisfied. Blessed are you that weep now, for you shall laugh.'[6]

We may take these to be genuine Jesus-sayings, not the fruits of subsequent paraphrase. The three quoted statements comprehensively represent the man, and those he is addressing are the lowest social classes.

In Max Weber's writings[7] on the economic ethics of the world

religions (in this case his work on Judaism) there is a useful account
of the economic and social conditions of Palestine, including an
account of how the classes were divided. Between the town fathers
and the established farmers, some of them free but others tied in
one way or another by rent or service as tenant farmers, who farmed
corn, fruit, wine and cattle, and the free, camel-breeding Bedouin,
there stood another group common until recent times to all
countries of the Mediterranean world: the semi-nomadic, small
cattle (sheep and goats) breeders. Economic and political power in
such a system rested fundamentally with the rich land-owners who
lived in Jerusalem gathering and spending their rents, a system
that laid the farmers open to usury practised on them by their
landlords. During the last pre-Christian centuries there emerged
in the towns a type of petit bourgeoisie and from this class came
the brotherhood of Pharisees. As a class, these people had nothing
to do with the farmers nor with the semi-nomadic sheep breeders.
These in turn paid little heed to the dictates of the teachers of the
law (there were several hundred of these detailed prescriptions for
the conduct of everyday life alone). In contrast, many artisans –
for example, blacksmiths, carpenters, shoemakers, woodcutters –
were more or less sympathetic to the strict and reverential attitude
the Jew was required to have towards the law. Several rabbis came
from this group, among them Saul, later to become the Apostle
Paul.

But the overall economic situation should not be overlooked in
the course of these considerations. Here there is a rule of thumb
that is also valid for all other pre-industrial societies: an annual
per capita income of not less than $50 and not more than $200.
The *per capita* income in the Roman Empire (population 100
million), of which Palestine was then a part, has been put at $100
a year, which would be about the level now prevailing in present-
day Indonesia. Out of every hundred people, ninety-two would
have worked on the land, and their standard of living would have
been very low. Whereas in modern industrial societies the majority
of the population will belong to the middle classes, the situation in
earlier times was quite different. Then there was a very broadly-
based lower class, a smaller urban, bourgeois middle class, and the

the relatively tiny upper class that kept its riches secure within a small number of families. Among the Jews at the time of Jesus the latter class consisted of the aristocracy of the blood and the priestly nobility, both resident in Jerusalem. It was from this class, the leaders of the people, that the Sanhedrin, mentioned in the New Testament, recruited its members.

Bearing all this in mind, it is not difficult to visualize the constitution of Jesus's first audience: piece-workers, tenant farmers, itinerant shepherds, fishermen, perhaps a few artisans, and some women and children. There will have been many among his listeners quite capable of detecting learned or even patronizing condescension. But of Jesus they said that he taught 'as one who had authority, and not as their scribes'.[8]

This introduces an excellent criterion, namely the conventions of speech. Within one and the same language the various social classes equip themselves with differing codes, the one more simple or more complicated than the other, according to the standard of education achieved. The scribes would have had a larger vocabulary – which is where it all starts. Words, too, are riches, not just houses and cattle.

He who has a large vocabulary but little money or property we call an intellectual. It is very probable that this type first emerged among the Jews, in the form of the rabbi (only in Medieval India is a comparable situation to be found).

'Where your treasure is, there will your heart be also', said Jesus.[9] The heart of the learned man throughout the ages has been with his vocabulary, and the visible expression of this love of learning is the library. Clay tablets, scrolls, codices – since man learned to write, and more especially since he developed an alphabet, it has been possible to store up words, and whoever could read had access to these treasuries.

Like Buddha and Socrates, Jesus himself left us no writings. He did not share the intellectual's passion for words: 'I thank thee, Father . . . that thou hast hidden these things from the wise and understanding, and revealed them to babes.'[10]

And there again are the poor, this time understood as the educationally deprived.

Jesus in bad company

Although the rabbis and Pharisees do not belong to the highest class, but rather constitute some sort of plebeian intellectual group[11] equipped with a basically bourgeois ethic, they are still too far above Jesus on the social scale. His sermons are not for them. The advice that he himself gave to take the lowest place among the guests at table[12] he followed scrupulously in the most general sense of the parable. Measured in terms of property and education, his social position was way down at the bottom.

A BRIGHTER FUTURE

Matthew tells us that the poor have good news preached to them[13] and this *Evangelium* (which means 'good news') was in the first instance: You will laugh and you will eat your fill.

Among those to whom weeping came more readily than laughing, and whose appetite was rarely satisfied, such news was bound to go down well and was easily understood by even the dullest intelligence. The misery would soon come to an end, the beggars would feast with Abraham, good times lay ahead, and the last would be first.[14]

In the new world order all this would become reality, and it was this world order that Jesus spoke of as the kingdom of God. Indeed, he spoke as though it were already at hand: 'But if it is by the finger of God that I cast out demons, then the kingdom of God has come upon you.'[15] But, of course, not yet in its full glory. So Jesus taught the poor a prayer that later the rich also learned by heart, even if their desire for change was hardly as strong: 'Thy kingdom come.'[16]

And then: 'Give us each day our daily bread.'

But the latter request presupposes an almost impossibly absurd state of mind in that it assumes a willingness to cease storing food, building property, and amassing capital. Only the man who really does live from hand to mouth can pray literally for his daily bread; one in short who, with Jesus, takes no thought for the morrow: 'Therefore do not be anxious about tomorrow, for tomorrow will be anxious for itself'.[17] Such an attitude can still be found today among the lowest social classes, where feasts are celebrated as they occur, to the horror of those who have learned to save – save in time of plenty and want not in time of need.

And yet Jesus attributes to the economical a quality that they would least expect, namely stupidity. Luke tells a parable: 'The land of a rich man brought forth plentifully; and he thought to himself, "What shall I do, for I have nowhere to store my crops?" And he said, "I will do this: I will pull down my barns, and build larger ones; and there I will store all my grain and my goods. And I will say to my soul, Soul, you have ample goods laid up for many years; take your ease, eat, drink, be merry." But God said to him, "Fool! This night your soul is required of you; and the things you have prepared, whose will they be?" '[18]

Better, then, not to save at all: 'Do not lay up for yourselves treasures on earth, where moth and rust consume and where thieves break in and steal.'[19] Rather should we 'consider the lilies of the field, how they grow; they neither toil nor spin; yet I tell you, even Solomon in all his glory was not arrayed like one of these. . . . But seek first his kingdom . . . and all these things shall be yours as well.'

'The economic naïvety with which Jesus handled the themes of work and food in his preaching is frequently to be observed.'[20] It would be very easy to consider Jesus thereby discredited, as though he were some sort of mixed-up fanatic ready to promise his listeners the skies. But then how would one explain the phenomenon that Arnold Toynbee observed, namely the amazing response Jesus found among the poor[21] – for instance, among the people of Rome whose poor listened sympathetically to his message in spite of the world's failure to end? Or the previously mentioned appearance of the poor Jesus among the *poverellos* of the thirteenth century, for example, in Francis of Assisi's Christmas celebrations in the Greccio woods in 1223? Then there is the presence of Jesus among the hostile peasant farmers of Sicily, as on one occasion reported in a newspaper interview with a Sicilian farmer's wife in 1893:

'*Question*: How do you stand with your priests?

'*Answer*: Jesus was a true socialist.[22] But the priests do not represent him well, especially when they are usurers. In the confessional they said that socialists are excommunicated. But we answered that they were mistaken.'

In 1936, referring to burning Malaga, an old Spanish anarchist said that 'not one stone will be left upon another'.[23]

Words that come straight from the thirteenth chapter of Mark's gospel. Jesus's continuing influence among the wretched of the earth takes place, then, in spite of his manifest error regarding the imminent end. Here one detects a current running through the lower layers of Christianity that has endured century after century and that is hardly in agreement with the official Jesus of the world Churches.

And this current has a richer life in it than is to be found even among theologians of the rank of Rudolf Bultmann, who sees the strained situation of the first Christians with regard to civic duties as no more than a passing phase, thus rendering Jesus more or less harmless and preserving him safely within the bosom of the bourgeois middle class. What Bultmann has to say about a happier future is best quoted literally: 'In the last analysis, however, the future can never, as in Gnosticism, be conceived in fantastic cosmic terms, despite all the apocalyptic imagery which has found its way into the New Testament. It can only be understood in the light of God's grace as the permanent futurity of God which is always there before man arrives, wherever it be, even in the darkness of death.'[24]

The Grimm brothers said something to this effect in the story of the hare and the hedgehog, where the hedgehog says to the hare: 'Here I am already.'

THAT IMPOSTOR

Matthew tells us that after his death the Jewish authorities referred to Jesus as 'that impostor'.[25] And Luke reports that when Jesus was up before Pilate these same authorities said that 'he stirs up the people'.[26] John also hands down to us a critical voice when he records the comment that 'he is leading the people astray'.[27]

In the gospels Jesus is found amidst great crowds of people who follow him around shouting their enthusiasm, and on one occasion they actually wanted to crown him king. Then again we read of how he would retreat to some remote place with only his disciples for company. Mention is made of Jesus's compassion: 'I have compassion on the crowd,'[28] but we also hear of him cursing in tones of great bitterness. After preaching in the towns around Lake Genessaret he warns them of trouble to come.[29] He is disappointed because they do not listen to him. He speaks sadly to Jerusalem, the capital city: ' . . . and you would not.'

Jesus compared his contemporaries with children who cannot agree about what games to play: 'But to what shall I compare this generation? It is like children sitting in the market places and calling to their playmates, "We have piped to you, and you did not dance; we wailed, and you did not mourn." '[30]

No one can make headway with these people, neither the ascetic John the Baptist nor Jesus, whose way of life was so unbiased. Though Jesus is obviously popular, his popularity provokes more than one response. His intentions in the Sermon on the Mount are clear enough and yet the response to it is fragmentary and ambiguous. John's gospel, which in general is deeply pessimistic with regard to mass appeal, highlights the situation in Jesus's somewhat anguished appeal immediately after the feeding of the five thousand: 'Truly, truly, I say to you, you seek me, not because you saw signs, but because you ate your fill of the loaves.'[31] And then there is the famous saying when Jesus was being tempted by the devil: 'Man shall not live by bread alone'[32] (which in fact comes from Deuteronomy).

This is a clear condemnation of what has been called welfare communism, attempts to fob people off with just enough to keep them going. There's more at stake than the daily bread, as the poor are so often made aware. Prosperity alone does not bring goodness with it.

The latter is much more likely to be achieved by offering help to whoever at any particular moment needs it, and the humbler the person is the better: 'Truly, I say to you, as you did it to one of the least of these my brethren, you did it to me.'[33]

'It is central to the preaching of love that what love requires is not impossible of achievement, even in the long run.'[34] Had Jesus been no more than a latter-day fanatic who went around promising the poor heaven on earth, the eternal hunting-grounds of the religious dream country, he need not have bothered about the preaching of a message of love. There is no sign in the love he preached of the profound disinterest that characterizes those willing to wait passively for the great day of judgment. On the contrary, his preaching is characterized by genuine enthusiasm and sincerity, and a morality anxious to put into effect at once the instructions it contains: 'Go and do likewise.'[35]

And Jesus addressed himself always to the poor. When a rich man shows enthusiasm for Jesus's advice, he is told that he must first get rid of what he has: 'Sell your possessions, and give alms.'[36] Nowhere does Jesus recommend or attach value to social climbing. He could find no kind word for what the sociologists call 'upward mobility'. Indeed, he calls for the reverse, in other words the social descent of the man who has sold his possessions and now lives a simpler life, rejecting the social status he formerly had: 'Whoever humbles himself will be exalted.'[37]

Further: 'And calling to him a child, he put him in the midst of them, and said, "Truly, I say to you, unless you turn and become like children, you will never enter the kingdom of heaven. Whoever humbles himself like this child, he is the greatest in the kingdom of heaven." '[38]

Clearly the child in this parable is supposed to represent the lowest position on the social scale, though of course it is not intended that those who become like a child should necessarily be submissive and pliable (on this, more later).

In short: Jesus stood the traditional class system on its head, together with its attendant apparatus of status symbols and prestige-seeking. At the same time he urged people to take the lowest place. For those who are already there, 'labouring and heavy laden',[39] he advised a spirit of uninhibited readiness to help the very least of their brothers without showing any envy towards those who live it up higher up the ladder. And Jesus admonishes them: 'When you give a feast, invite the poor, the maimed, the lame, the blind.'[40]

It may be that Jesus was aware of the small chance there was of the poor not being envious.[41] In this respect it is possible that he learnt something from the reaction of his hearers. The extent of effective allegiance he was able to find among the people cannot now be assessed with any confidence. With more confidence, however, we may presume that Jesus had something quite paradoxical in mind as he sowed the seed of unrest among the lower classes – namely, the combination of radical dissatisfaction with an absence of envy.

Providence and heavenly dispensation in the unchanging condition of the poor, together with assurances of comfort through visions of a happier life in the next world, are as absent from Jesus's preaching as malice towards the lordliest of the land, as the psalmist called them. [42] The classical deceit of the priests[43] is to suggest a better life for the individual poor in the next world but never to call them collectively to anything better here and now. Because Jesus did direct their collective attention to the present, because he sided so unambiguously with the poor and ignored the traditional class divisions, the authorities had to accuse him of rebellion. The irony of this situation is that the accusation must fall flat in as far as Jesus never preached the expropriation of the rich, as we shall show, even though by doing so he could have curried great favour with the poor.

THE SOCIALLY DISADVANTAGED

With the help, for instance, of income statistics we are even able to count the number of those in this group.[44] In the United States, which has the highest *per capita* income in the world, 17.1 per cent of white households were classed as poor, as against 43.1 per cent of black households (1965 figures). Other economically deprived groups, apart from the blacks, are the farmers, the elderly, children, and the inhabitants of the Southern States. Two groups – elderly working people and, in general terms, all working women – suffer economic discrimination.

Average or mean values, as, for example, average annual income, constitute an important principle in the collection of such data. Anything above the mean income is considered to be above average, anything below it, below average. The sum of all annual incomes is divided by the number of wage-earners and the resultant arith-metical mean then serves as the norm. The process reflects what is called common sense – what is average is normal. Thus, for example, an average intelligence is regarded as a normal intelli-gence; exceptionally stupid or clever people occur infrequently. The final picture obtained from these statistics shows a high degree of symmetry, the number of the abnormally stupid cancelling out the number of the abnormally clever. But no neat norms exist for the stupid, the hunchbacked, the unnaturally fat, the dwarfs, the homosexuals, the not seriously crippled, alcoholics, slum-dwellers, and criminals. Nor for America's blacks, farmers, or elderly. All these groups deviate from the sacred average, that determinant of social morality. But they are all unhappy minorities, even if many of them are just able to make do economically.

The United States has reached a point at which poverty could be banished at one stroke. Raising the income of each individual and every household above the basic minimum would cost the United States of America about ten thousand million dollars a year. That is no more than 2 per cent of the gross national product, less than 10 per cent of total tax receipts, and about one fifth of the cost of the national defence programme. But the step is not taken. And even if in God's own country and within the foreseeable future this poverty were to be lifted, the misery of those who in some other way deviate from the norm would continue. Even with just enough to live on – that is, technically not poor – the lonely elderly are poor enough.

We are now back with the sad and weeping people whom Jesus addressed, the girls who never got married, the women deserted by their husbands; with those whom no revolution has helped. The categories of social class do not contain them and money alone does not make them happy.

The least of the brethren does not necessarily have to be the poorest in economic terms. The sermon of love has nothing what-ever to do with the greatest good of the greatest number. Jesus was thinking of those who are burdened with anxiety; not of the average consumer but precisely the unfortunate minorities – including the hungry, of course, but not forgetting the maimed, the lame, and the blind. These people are regarded as the norm, and on the day of judgment will be seen as such, not the average man. Whoever, then, belongs to the 'little flock' of the deprived, no matter what the nature of the deprivation, his is the kingdom, as we learn from Luke.[45]

We are entitled to speak in Jesus's case of a wholly fresh approach to those who, socially or economically, do not fit into society's norm, and to the deprived minorities of society. Jesus challenges society to come to grips with its minorities and to worry less about its average citizens.

In all this we can detect in Jesus the rudiments of a fundamental critique of society, an attitude of defiance towards the social complex as a whole: 'This generation is an evil generation.'[46] Luke makes it plain that Jesus said this to the crowds gathering around him. Jesus never soft-soaped anyone, nor would he necessarily side with the majority; democracy was not of itself a way into his heart. Nowadays, were one to characterize the direction of Jesus's energies, one would look for him among the homeless: 'Foxes have holes, and the birds of the air have nests; but the Son of man has nowhere to lay his head.'[47]

Or perhaps he would be found in the so-called twilight or underworld where those live who are in permanent conflict with the prevailing laws. In Jesus's day this meant the tax gatherers whom we discussed earlier; in other words, the sinners pure and simple. Jesus showed them a degree of sympathy that was downright provocative. They, of all people, march straight into heaven, safely ahead of the leaders of the people: 'The tax collectors and the harlots go into the kingdom of God before you.'[48]

And this, according to Matthew, was said to the chief priests and elders.

PRODIGAL SON: PUNISHMENT IS NOT MANDATORY

In two of Jesus's parables the actual message is spelt out in numbers: 'What man of you, having a hundred sheep, if he has lost one of them, does not leave the ninety-nine in the wilderness, and go after the one which is lost, until he finds it? . . . Or what woman, having ten silver coins, if she loses one coin, does not light a lamp and sweep the house and seek diligently until she finds it?'[49]

The emphasis is in one case on a tenth, in the other on a mere hundredth. If we want to take it all literally, then it appears that Jesus is interested in extremely small units, indeed in what one could only call negligible quantities. For it goes without saying that one would look for a sheep or a coin sooner than one would look for a man who had fallen on hard times.

As, for example, the prodigal son in the famous parable. The point is that the errant son is not punished, that no sanctions are brought against him. But though from one point of view the affair is carried off so mildly, the elder son, who had in fact behaved himself, shot off in an opposite direction, turning his father's mildness into the cause of a fundamental estrangement between them. Something universal can be detected in this estrangement, and certainly the penitent son is convinced of it as he anxiously prepares his plea for forgiveness: 'Treat me as one of your hired servants.'

A subtlety of the parable is that in the event he never actually makes this particular plea for just punishment; one does not always have to be punished. In this case – and remember that he only returned home at all because he was in dire need – a feast was given in honour of the wretched man: 'Let us eat and make merry.'

This then was an exception to the less happy disciplinary measures applied to miscreants and deviants since Adam and Eve. The exception is also somewhat subversive of law and order: a father spares the rod. Whatever next – with all those 'extortioners', and 'adulterers' around!

This list is taken from another parable,[50] in this case one about a Pharisee praying piously in the temple while casting sidelong glances at a tax collector who had also come up to pray. A tax collector in those days was looked on as a common criminal, a 'white-collar criminal' as one might say today. No Robin Hood, but a man for whom charity begins at home. But in this story he happens to be disgusted with himself.

'I tell you,' said Jesus, 'this man went down to his house justified rather than the other.' No reasons are given for preferring the penitent wretch to the pious do-gooder. But the message is clear.

We can be certain that the Pharisees (*perushim* – the 'set apart', those who hold themselves distant) understood Jesus's censure very well. For it was precisely within their brotherhood that all social contact was avoided with those who did not live strictly within the requirements of the Torah. This led to a contrast between the elect and the ordinary people, the ignorant who not knowing the law did not keep it. The contrast was driven to extremes and very nearly reached the point of ritual caste segregation. Here, then, we have the sect.[51]

That this tendency towards segregation from non-nationals was a determining factor for the Jews of the Diaspora and that even in pre-Christian times the strong anti-Semitism present in antiquity was a reaction to this attitude – all of this is tangential to the purpose of this book.

Nevertheless, one can see Jesus's social direction very clearly if one is aware of this background of caste and party in the Jewish society of his day. When the Jews as a people raised ethnic arguments and prejudices against the Samaritans then living in central Palestine, Jesus at once sided with the Samaritans – and was immediately abused as one of them.[52] When the Pharisees shut themselves off from those unfamiliar with the law, there was no question as to where Jesus's sympathies lay, and he showed them clearly.

In effect then, Jesus rejected a fundamental human characteristic – the labelling and pigeon-holing of social types alongside and in opposition to one another. The pleasure that social groups obtain from despising one another, he found in turning to the despised, the ignored, and the forgotten.

In the gospels this is called mercy. Put more precisely – following the Greek original – a movement that wells up from one's inner self, from one's very entrails. The father in the parable of the prodigal son, the good Samaritan,[53] the king in the story of the unmerciful servant[54] – these were all moved by the same impulse. As was Jesus himself when faced with a hungry crowd, or a mother whose son had died;[55] his concern is always with the person for whom at any given moment things go badly.

Concern is also shown for groups of people with whom one

would not normally have any contact: 'And if you salute only your brethren, what more are you doing than others?'

And finally, the ultimate: 'Love your enemies.'[56]

Jesus is developing a somewhat unusual sociogram.[57] Those addressed are asked to give first preference precisely to those groups they have thought of least, and if at all then only as enemies. Thus the forgotten and the enemy are pushed into the normative position: we are asked to consider them and to see them as base in our consideration of others. Social behaviour is to be determined not by élites or majorities but rather by the poor, the mournful, the hungry. As far as Jesus is concerned, these are the people that matter and it is therefore to them that he turns. For one's way of thought to proceed from the opposite end of the social scale flies in the face of the total experience of human social history; it is contrary to the social experience of all civilizations in all ages. It was also the start of something that much later, in the French Revolution, was to be proclaimed as *fraternité*, and later still as the classless society in which the proletariat would act as agents for a happier future. The collapse of the true Jesus in all subsequent history therefore remains a fact. What he might have brought about was the presence in societies touched by Christianity of men whose avowed purpose in life was goodness practised daily amidst the stink of misery and disease. At least this has led to the giving of alms as something good and acceptable, even if it is more often than not used as a relatively cheap heavenly travel voucher for those who live easy lives.

It has to be admitted that the cocoons of self-interest men have wrapped themselves in have grown no less impregnable since Jesus's time. His attempt to bring about an aggression-reducing change of direction through a movement downwards has not come off; the medicine he prescribed has never been taken.

Chapter 7
The very stones would cry out

It is not just because of his beard that Che Guevara (d. 1967) reminds many people of Jesus. He was an astute man, a *guerrillero* and doctor, with gentle eyes. After Cuba's successful revolution he no longer wanted to stay on as a minister but instead, taking leave of his family, went into the forests of another country. His little daughter didn't recognize him. In fact this gentle, determined man might well have been more dangerous to the happy few had he stayed on in a position of power where his unwavering, premeditated anger might have been more effective than the gesticulations of those who made great speeches.

When things go wrong for the powerful of this world they usually take up arms. All four gospels tell of Jesus's spectacular entry into Jerusalem, surrounded by his followers, on the occasion of the, for him, fatal Easter ceremonies.[1] Some scholars have seen in this event a signal that Jesus wanted to lead a *coup*. But in historical terms this is neither here nor there, as we cannot now know what Jesus had in mind as he and his followers travelled to Jerusalem for the feast of the Passover. But in Luke's account of what happened words are attributed to Jesus that, as a sign of the indignation he felt, one would unwillingly ascribe to the hand of a subsequent editor. When some of the Pharisees appealed to Jesus to rebuke his disciples for acclaiming him so vigorously, Jesus replied: 'I tell you, if these were silent, the very stones would cry out.'

THE MAN OF STRIFE

No man, unless he be of disturbed mind, lives willingly in a situation of permanent conflict with the ruling authorities. But if in such a situation, then one could justifiably bemoan one's lot, as for instance Jeremiah did: 'Woe is me, my mother, that you bore me, a man of strife and contention to the whole land!... I did not sit in the company of merrymakers.'[2]

What we need to examine is the cause of contention in Jesus's case, the object of his anger, the reason why he did not make merry. As discussed in earlier chapters, his attitude to the temple religion, the family as institution, and the class system would have sufficed on their own to arouse the suspicions of the guardians of law and order; and that would be true of any society known to us, not just of the Jews of those times.

In addition we must also take into account the historically well-attested divide between Jesus and what one might call the dominant Torah piety, by which one means the social conventions of his times securely anchored within religion and culture: it was this antipathy that led directly to his death, as has already been discussed in an earlier chapter.

There remains then the question of Jesus's rebellion against the division of power and the chains of command in the political sphere, including their acceptance by his fellow Jews.

One could start with the negative observation that Jesus was no putsch leader nor a (national) revolutionary armed with a detailed action programme. Neither was he a social reformer, and nor do those types of the pre-political social rebels – as described by Eric J. Hobsbawm[3] – do him justice. There is no sign in Jesus of a political action directed at the attainment of temporal power.[4]

And yet there is something within him smouldering fiercely: 'I came to cast fire upon the earth; and would that it were already kindled!'[5]

And he had the weapons, too: 'Do not think that I have come to bring peace on earth; I have not come to bring peace, but a sword.'[6]

Jesus also shows signs of the ruthlessness often found among those determined to achieve something: 'No one who puts his hand to the plough and looks back is fit for the kingdom of God.'[7] And to a disciple who wanted time off so that he could bury his dead father: 'Follow me, and leave the dead to bury their own dead.'[8] With this fierce sideswipe Jesus impatiently rejects a concern for the dead that is as old as man. Jesus is without reverence; not even death is sacred.

'In the case of great young men, rods which measure consistency, inner balance, or proficiency, simply do not fit the relevant dimensions.'[9] It is important to remember this so that one does not through excess caution undervalue or depreciate the fundamentally rebellious, indeed militant, side of Jesus. It is precisely this attitude of cautious neutralization, cultivated among others by diplomats and theologians, that Jesus so firmly rejected: 'So, because you are lukewarm, and neither cold nor hot, I will spew you out of my mouth.'[10]

YOUR ANGER IS TOO SLOW

Before Jesus was born, his mother sang a song of defiance that was full of brave confidence: 'He has put down the mighty from their thrones, and exalted those of low degree.'[11]

The 'he' here is not the God of the monarchists, for the 'Magnificat', which this sentence comes from, is full of the old prophetic spirit of rebellion against the arrogance of the powerful. God 'looses the bonds of kings, and binds a waistcloth on their loins' – thus Job in uninhibited mood.[12]

'Early on, Israel's prophets took precautions to prevent any of their kings from assuming a divine aura, as so frequently happened among neighbouring powers, as for instance with the Egyptians. And it was from Egypt that the Jews fled with Moses, who had killed an overseer. Yahweh began by threatening Pharaoh with plagues, and then the iron God of Sinai became through Moses the God of liberation, the God of the exodus from slavery.'[13] Those who danced around the golden calf were soon brought low – you cannot serve God and Mammon. That was in the former nomadic times. Then the Jews settled in Canaan, tilled the soil, established vineyards; trade developed, and so did social contrasts.

97

Money brought corruption in its wake, even among the judges of the people, and this gave rise to the demand that a king be set over them 'to govern us like all the nations'.

Very unwillingly, the old God of the desert acceded to this request and in Gilgal somewhere around the year 1030 BC Saul became their first king. But opposition to royal rule persisted and some three hundred years later the prophet Hosea complained: 'Every evil of theirs is in Gilgal.'[14]

By then the monarchy's finest days – under Solomon (*c.* 970-30 BC) – were over and the prophets were up in arms. They even appear in the chronicles of the kings – Elijah against Ahab, and Elisha against Joram – all in the ninth century BC and against a background of starvation.[15] So far they had not developed any detailed message but they were implacably opposed to the corruption they witnessed, an opposition fostered by the persecution they suffered as prophets.

Ultimately their critique was written down and became a part of sacred literature. It was Elijah who, together with Moses, appeared at Jesus's side during the transfiguration on Mount Tabor[16] as a significant representative of a subversive ethos and a watchdog against social decay.

'Initially the prophetic programme was concerned with the removal of new practices introduced during the time of the monarchy, particularly those within the political sphere; militarism and its trappings, the royal treasures, the harems of foreign princesses and their cults, the royal favourites in official positions, the people forced to work in the fields and on building projects.'[17] These were acts of restoration harking back to their former nomadic culture which had managed without a bureaucracy. And then on to an attack against socio-political conditions including onslaughts against bribery, miscarriages of justice, the oppression of the poor, and avarice generally. In short, these were the reproaches of the pre-capitalist common people against court officials and patrician families.

'Between roughly 750 and 600 BC the prophets were agitating in the marketplace or at the town gate, especially in Jerusalem, and their target was always those in power. From time to time the core

of their message was written down and distributed by friends or
followers – they thus became the first pamphleteers in history.'[18]
Their primary concern was with questions of foreign policy for
their little country was having a hard time of it between the major
powers of Egypt and Assyria.

In this context we can see clearly that in none of their political
interventions did the prophets show any interest in direct political
action: Yahweh alone was in a position to make things different,
his anger was decisive, even when he made people wait: Jeremiah
finds Yahweh too longsuffering.[19]

'In spite of sharp anti-monarchist attitudes and a manifest
antipathy towards the upper classes, the prophets never tried to
wrest power from them, as revolutionary movements usually do.'[20]
Instead, they constructed massive images of a world at peace[21] in
which swords are beaten into ploughshares and spears into knives
for the vine. A world in which the wolf lies down with the lamb and
the lion eats straw.

'Only the momentum generated by the prophets made Israel to
this unique extent into a people that waited in constant expectation.'[22] And while waiting, no truce was made – at least not by the
prophets – with the world around them; neither can they be
accused of a fundamental or otherworldly indifference towards the
true balance of power.

This is evident enough from the words of the 'Magnificat'
mentioned above. Whoever gave us the 'Magnificat' in its present
form as a chain of quotations from the prophetic tradition was
anxious to include himself, as a Judeo-Christian, within this
tradition. To put all this in more general terms: the early Christian
tradition that found expression in the four gospels saw Jesus as a
prophet: 'A great prophet has arisen among us! and God has
visited his people!'[23]

But this of itself still tells us nothing about Jesus's actual purpose.
We know something about the social, political, intellectual, and
economic climate that made him the man he was, and of the zeal
and enthusiasm of the last days that dominated among the baptist
groups on the Jordan (among which there perhaps circulated a very
early version of the 'Magnificat' that Luke later adopted). It will

have been one of these groups[24] that John led, and it is possible that Jesus himself was among them for a while before he appeared in public.

A study of this situation could at best provide us with a little atmosphere with which to back up our understanding of the circumstances that made Jesus a rebel. It is as though one were to enquire through whom Beethoven learned counterpoint. The magnitude and significance of Jesus even as a rebel will not be grasped merely by seeing him as the best disciple of John the Baptist or even of the angry old prophets.

DO NOT FEAR

'There is nothing a man fears more than the touch of the unknown. He wants to see what is reaching towards him, and to be able to recognize or at least classify it. – The touch to which one resigns oneself because all resistance appears hopeless – and particularly so as regards the future – has, in our society, become the arrest. The moment of seizing, which is decisive amongst animals as well as amongst men, has always created the strongest impression on men. . . . Power discharges commands like a hail of magical arrows. – Commands are older than speech. If this were not so, dogs could not understand them. – Beneath all commands glints the harshness of the death sentence.'[25]

Those sentences, extracted from Elias Canetti's book, expose the dangerous face of power. If Jesus had not been seized and arrested, condemned and executed, then it would not be necessary to consider this aspect of life in our discussion of Jesus's social behaviour. But in the event Jesus experienced to the full the danger of man's power over man.

One might ask if Jesus accepted all this more or less passively, as fate perhaps, or as the consequence and cost of his desire for change and of his attitude to the Torah. And it is a fact that one cannot establish in the historical Jesus a direct, fundamental and critical line of agitation directed against power relationships.

'If Jesus was not an active political leader . . . desired no social revolution . . . if he was far from any idea of self-aggrandizement, and his whole life was an act of obedience to God's will, his conduct becomes hard to understand. For by violence (cleansing of the temple, creation of a movement among the people) he provoked violence against himself. What he suffered was the consequence of his act. In all this there is a flavour of militancy which is also unmistakable in other manifestations of his personality.'[26]

It should be remembered that Jesus saw the imminent onset of God's dominion (in place of its human counterpart) as something that would be controlled from above and not as a movement to be actively pursued here below. One can and should adjust oneself to this fact by accepting Jesus's call to spiritual conversion and generally taking trouble to interpret the signs of the times correctly.[27] The concealed knife carried by the political radicals of those days – they were called Zealots[28] – remained out of the question for Jesus, even if, as has often been supposed, Judas Iscariot may have been a Zealot, and a certain Simon in Luke's list of apostles is explicitly numbered as a member of this group.[29] Jesus was most certainly not the leader of a political conspiracy – on this point modern scholarship is almost unanimous.

Strange though it may sound to those unfamiliar with the history of those times, Jesus might conceivably have had better chances with the Jewish authorities had he in fact been a conspirator-Messiah. There was a conspirator after him called Bar Cochba (=son of the stars) who in AD 132 led a revolt against the Romans and who was hailed as the Messiah by Akiba, the most respected and learned rabbi of his day. For though Bar Cochba rebelled against Rome, he did so for nationalistic and revisionist reasons, which means that he did it for the Jewish Church-State, including its priestly caste. The latter, consequently, was only too willing to bless his efforts.

In fact Jesus lived in the last national period of Judaism which began in 63 BC with Pompey's entry into Jerusalem, and ended in AD 135 with the collapse of Bar Cochba's revolt. (Not until the State of Israel was founded on 14 May 1948 were the Jews once again to have a country of their own.) But Jesus's outlook was not determined by nationalist hopes. 'He never speaks of a political

Messiah who will destroy the enemies of Israel, of the establishment of a Jewish world empire, the gathering of the twelve tribes, of peace and prosperity in the land, or anything of that kind.'[30] All this is very significant precisely in this period of desperate but frustrated popular uprisings.[31] Jesus was neither a national nor a revisionist Messiah, that much is clear.

Shorn of the possibility of establishing a coalition of one sort or another, and given his failure to manipulate politically the popular following available to him at least in Galilee, he would appear to emerge as little more than a harmless fanatic whose mad ideas were of small concern to those in power. That this was not so, that Jesus's message had a very definite impact among the authorities, is shown by the fact that he was finally executed, an end that was undoubtedly desired in leading circles.

As we have already discussed in an earlier chapter, this was up to a point understandable given Jesus's way-out, indeed criminal, attitude to the cultural and religious conventions of his society. That in addition to all that Jesus directed his critical attention to the power complex itself with the purpose of drawing its sting can only be shown indirectly.

For instance, there is a saying reliably attributed to Jesus that indicates the direction of his thoughts: 'I tell you, my friends, do not fear those who kill the body, and after that have no more that they can do.'[32]

'If we would master power we must face command openly and boldly, and search for means to deprive it of its sting' (Canetti).[33] The urgency with which one looks at this point for the slightest indication that Jesus ever defied naked power can be explained through an experience that neither Marx nor Freud had, namely the fifty-five million dead as a result of the Second World War, a war unleashed by one power-mad individual. The helplessness of the great Churches in the face of these events strengthens one's zeal.

The empirically observed connection between the will to kill and the exercise of dictatorial power, between aggression and authoritarian behaviour, cannot be brushed aside with Freud's death wish (which in any case is controversial) nor with Marx's comment that death is the harsh victory of the species over the individual.[34]

In Jesus's remark about death quoted above from Luke's gospel, death is not meant as a natural event but as a killing, something brought about by man. Was Paul showing his awareness of this when he wrote of Jesus that death no longer had power over him? For Paul knew that Jesus's death was no natural one. Was he saying that Jesus had opened up a possibility of a victory that could draw death's sting?[35] That the healing factor came precisely from the rejection of the survival-at-all-costs approach? According to Canetti[36] this latter, namely the ruthless will to survive, is the very heart and kernel of power.

Looked at through modern eyes the problem could be said to be how to extract the dictator's fangs without in the process initiating a fresh accumulation of power. Whether or not Jesus saw things this way, we cannot tell for certain. The fearlessness in the face of power, including the death of the body, which Jesus perhaps wanted to bring about is an indication, not a proof.

YOU HAVE HEARD HIS BLASPHEMY

The result is similar when we come to assess Jesus's attitude to the highest authority, God himself.

'The Jewish God is a patriarchal monarch.'[37] 'Thus the conception of a holy nation with God as its King was in the peculiar form of a Church-State.'[38] At the time of Jesus the ordinary Jew justified the nature of his people's power structures on the basis of their ratification by God. The Roman occupying power, naturally, had nothing to do with this process – but then it was not that power that arrested Jesus.

Not even the prophets in their rebellion against the mighty of the land came anywhere near the sovereignty of God: 'For my thoughts are not your thoughts, neither are your ways my ways, says the Lord.'[39] 'The interest in every single soul, evinced by the God of the Bible, the tenacity with which he remembers and cares for each, may be taken as the model of all who wield power.'[40] Only once was Yahweh attacked from a position within Jewish piety, and that was in the Book of Job. Job's case, however, was not without certain precedents in which revolt against God is implied in the Bible – such as the serpent in paradise[41] with its highly inflammatory 'you will be like God', not to mention Cain, whose case has already been described. 'Until Dostoevsky and Nietzsche, rebellions were directed exclusively at that cruel and capricious divinity who without convincing reason preferred Abel's sacrifice to Cain's and thereby provoked the first murder.'[42] The author of the Book of Job (around 450 BC?) has his wretched main character (whom he borrowed from an old legend) ask God to explain himself: 'Let me know why thou dost contend against me.'

And then comes an attack on God's arbitrariness: 'It is all one; therefore I say, he destroys both the blameless and the wicked. When disaster brings sudden death, he mocks at the calamity of the innocent.' And finally, wholly unambiguous reference to the division of power between God and man: 'If it is a contest of strength, behold him! If it is a matter of justice, who can summon him?'

God's answer to Job, spoken, inevitably, from the midst of a storm of thunder and lightning, is that of offended majesty: 'Where were you when I laid the foundation of the earth? . . . Have you commanded the morning since your days began, and caused the dawn to know its place . . . ?' A whole catalogue of similarly rhetorical questions reduces Job to silence: 'What shall I answer thee? I lay my hand on my mouth.'

In return Job is at once rewarded. Yahweh reverses his fate and increases twofold all that he had formerly possessed. With this, the old order is nicely re-established and Job is restored to favour as a patient sufferer; and the only words of his now quoted are: 'The Lord gave, and the Lord has taken away; blessed be the name of the Lord.' Even the concluding reconciliation between God and Job remains within the traditional division of power, indeed confirms it.[43] 'An act of mercy is a very high and concentrated expression of power, for it presupposes condemnation. There can be no mercy unless there has first been condemnation.'[44]

Nevertheless those passages of the Book of Job that are unsympathetic to the traditional concept of God have also been preserved and now form a part of the official Jewish and Christian canon. Astonishing here is that an unacceptable degree of arbitrariness is found in God himself, together with unaccountable moods and destructive fits of anger; God, it appears, could be extremely jealous and sensitive.[45]

But, as Jaspers concludes,[46] Jesus, unlike Job, does not remonstrate against the arbitrariness of God, against the monarchic lord of heaven and earth and his unfathomable decrees. And yet he was arrested by the Jewish authorities as a heretic and blasphemer. The statement Mark puts in the mouth of the high priest on the occasion of the (historically probably fictitious) trial of Jesus before the Sanhedrin expresses the point excellently: 'You have heard his blasphemy.'[47]

For Jesus's delivery to Pilate on the grounds that he was a political agitator was a mere pretext. Jesus was arrested as an enemy of the law and executed by the Romans as an enemy of the emperor.[48] But if Jesus was in fact a heretic (and it is clear that he was) then we have to ask if he was not also such in reference to the God who existed in the imagination of his contemporaries.

Twice daily, morning and evening, every adult male Jew had to pray: 'Hear, O Israel: The Lord our God is one Lord: And thou shalt love the Lord thy God with thine heart, and with all thy soul, and with all thy might. . . . I am the Lord your God which brought you out of the land of Egypt, to be your God: I am the Lord your God.'[49]

The more than a thousand-year-old history of the origin of the Jewish concept of God is by now well known. We know that in its essence it is something unique. In it was removed in principle something that had been characteristic of archaic religiosity, namely the process of exchange and barter between men and their gods, a process that was achieved through magical and cultic procedures organized with the object of exorcizing and mollifying the unknown as this presented itself in the moods of nature, in sexual processes, in illness and in the need to die, and in the infringement of one's own rights and interests through the intrusion of those of others. The continuing existence of archaic elements in pre-Christian Judaism – as for instance in the temple worship – does not affect our case. For what mattered was that in and through the sacred writings Yahweh was present: they had the Torah, and this was their source of instruction. The Torah was to the Jews an organic system of reference to which they were bound. Its details found cohesion in the will of Yahweh, who remained faithful to his people and who was to be obeyed.

The Torah and the God of the Jews therefore belonged together. Every Jew was as much subject to the Torah as he was to God, and should anyone wish to introduce some fresh point of view then he must first show that what he had to say was in accordance with the Torah – by apt quotation and appropriate interpretation. This led to the emergence of schools of exegesis whose conclusions were later recorded, starting in the first post-Christian centuries in the Mishna, the Gemara, the Midrashim, and the Targum.

The same mentality can be observed in the gospels in the numerous references to the scriptures, also in the mouth of Jesus himself: 'And beginning with Moses and all the prophets, he interpreted to them in all the scriptures the things concerning himself.'[50]

As we now know, this has little to do with the real Jesus. Rather was it his way to let the written and oral Torah hold sway when and where he thought it ought, and to ignore it when he thought otherwise.[51] With the same self-appropriated sovereignty Jesus approached the God of the Torah, not out of stubbornness and rebelliousness, but as a son who had put all feelings of fear and stubbornness towards his father behind him, and felt able to approach him as an equal. In any event one looks in vain to Jesus for any sign of the obedience that characterized the pious Jew's attitude to the law-giving God, and it was in this attitude that the theologians and teachers of the law of Jesus's day detected something blasphemous; and in the circumstances they had good cause. But the Yahweh that pious Jews prayed to twice daily was not the Yahweh Jesus had blasphemed against; and he would naturally and without reservation have played his part in the religious services of his day. The effect of his rebellion was more indirect than otherwise, which in the circumstances says a lot for its maturity.

We can see then that Jesus was neither an atheist nor in Camus's sense an *homme révolté*; we shall not be able to define him in terms of Camus's literary categories.[52] But there can be no doubt but that he was a heretic, especially in respect of the concept of God dominant in the society of his day.

BORN EQUAL TO GOD

Jesus's disobedience with regard to the Torah God of his day is connected with an attitude that could very well be called trust in God: 'Or what man of you, if his son asks him for bread, will give him a stone? Or if he asks for a fish, will give him a serpent? If you then, who are evil, know how to give good gifts to your children, how much more will your Father who is in heaven give good things to those who ask him!'[53]

Here we are being asked to consider a kindly God, not the God who acts arbitrarily. But it is not always so: 'If your right eye causes you to sin, pluck it out and throw it away; it is better that you lose one of your members than that your whole body be thrown into hell.'[54]

Or: 'Do not fear those who kill the body but cannot kill the soul; rather fear him who can destroy both soul and body in hell.'[55]

Although there is no direct mention of the heavenly father, the threatening face of higher authority is very much there, and with singularly unpleasant consequences. Jesus does not banish fear of God in spite of his exhaustive preaching of trust in him; as before, the ambivalence of the heavenly father remains in evidence.

It is possible, but not reliably proven, that Jesus consciously conquered and mastered his deepest fears in the face of his punishing father in heaven. 'Jesus the man reveals himself in the purity of his soul and in his struggle with unexpected realities. This struggle culminates in no finished self-awareness or dogma. In the face of unexpected terrors, in the face of his mounting disappointment, all that was left him was his prayer: "Thy will be done".'[56]

What really took place in Jesus's mind in those night hours before his arrest on the Mount of Olives, let alone during the agony he endured on the cross, we shall never know. The small number of passages that do tell us something should not be left out of account without very good reason, but even if they are accepted as valid they are extremely difficult to interpret.

It is at least clear, however, that they contain no sign of filial obduracy.

But it is equally clear that neither do they contain what Paul was the first to call a sacrificial death,[57] through which Jesus, on behalf of all mankind, offers the Father atonement with his life in expiation of original sin. All such references, whether in Paul's writings or in the gospels, are in all probability the consequences of an interpretation of Jesus's passion presented by his disciples.

The Jesus theology of the first century conceives him in the first place as a man adopted by God, put to the test of suffering and death, and finally awakened on the third day and received into heaven. In other texts, Jesus is no longer awakened but rises from the dead of himself. In the end Jesus is himself God, his death a voluntary expiatory sacrifice of a priestly nature between God and man, which effects a general reconciliation. After a fierce ideological struggle within the Church, this tendency to equate Jesus and God the Father was accepted as dogma in the fourth century and contained within the expression of the *homoousia* (identity of essence) of the Son with the Father, in spite of vigorous attempts to make the Son subordinate to the Father. Paradoxically, it is possible that this development can in fact throw some light on the true Jesus, for he had himself already left behind any notion of subordination to the Almighty (and, as we have noted, without rancour), and by this very process had himself initiated what was later to become the enthronement of the man, Jesus.

A STRONG MAN'S HOUSE

Jesus as exorcist[58] belongs among the best-founded elements of tradition and therefore to historical reality. As exorcist Jesus pitted power against power, and his opponents attempted to explain this phenomenon in terms of a pact between him and the devil.[59] According to Mark, these opponents were the scribes, and as such they numbered among the leaders of the people. Their defence against Jesus is instructive, for their suggestion that Jesus himself was a devil was a projection mechanism[60] – from 'I hate you' comes a 'You hate me'. But the whole process presupposes that the scribes feel themselves threatened by Jesus. In effect, by arguing that Jesus's own power came to him through various devils, the scribes were themselves making a fairly obvious bid for power.

'Generally speaking, and from the point of view of cultural history, the exorcism of demons belongs to magical invocations of the frightening variety. The practice reaches right back to the first beginnings of civilization – devils are everywhere older than gods.'[61] 'Mastering demons is not only a part of primitive religion but an important element in all ancient religions, and it experienced a resurgence in late Judaism and in Hellenism. The time of Jesus found the practice at its height.'[62]

In Jesus's day, exorcizing devils and driving demons from the so-called possessed was, accordingly, a social function – rather like looking after the mentally sick in modern times. The object was to protect oneself against an inimical force, to ward off the possible destruction of the familiar world.

Belief in demons means: 'I have experienced the horrors of power which cares neither for my reason nor for my integrity.'[63] By coming to grips with the horrors of power (though without having official authorization to do so) Jesus places himself above the rabbis, who did not do what he had done and yet presented themselves as teachers in the art. But of Jesus the gospel says, quite accurately, that 'he taught them as one who had authority'.[64]

In the very moment in which he will undoubtedly have wanted to preach, another somewhat dark and unclear aspect of his personality comes to light. Something he himself said shows that it has to do with the assessing of power: 'But no one can enter a strong man's house and plunder his goods, unless he first binds the strong man; then indeed he may plunder his house.'[65]

Imagery of this type suggests something that could well belong to the very relevant question of the nature of Jesus's revolt against the powers of this world. One detects in Jesus the will to resist the forces of evil as represented by Satan or Beelzebul, the prince of demons, whom, the context shows, Jesus is referring to in the passage quoted. Jesus was also referring to Beelzebul when he said: 'I saw Satan fall like lightning from heaven.'[66]

What fell must previously have been up above, and will not have been without power. We see then that not everything that sits on high rules, and is powerful, not every authority is in Jesus's eyes *ipso facto* legitimate. More concretely: Jesus did not bother about official authorization for his activity but authorized himself. He was neither a priest nor an official teacher of the law; officially he wasn't even entitled to cast out devils. In short, he was a layman, and as such involved himself in the world of officialdom. The historical Jesus cannot be said to have had respect for authority.

IT SHALL NOT BE SO AMONG YOU

As might be imagined, Jesus was notorious for ignoring the sabbath rest. Social taboos as such meant nothing to him: 'The sabbath was made for man, not man for the sabbath.'[67]

Or: 'What man of you, if he has one sheep and it falls into a pit on the sabbath, will not . . . lift it out? Of how much more value is a man than a sheep!'[68]

These comments were undoubtedly addressed to the Pharisees, among others. But his opposition to them[69] is not considerable enough for us not to be able to discover something fundamental in his polemic against them. Jesus's anger is directed against making fetishes of social conventions, that is, against what the social psychologists call 'rigidity'.[70] By this is meant an attitude of all or nothing, a dependence on well-defined behaviour patterns, and a lack of imagination when it comes to finding answers to fresh situations.

'The converse of this, flexibility (not to be confused with instability), could then be described as the habit of thinking things out afresh in every new situation.'[71]

The connection between rigidity and authoritarian thinking can be regarded as certain; and it all starts in the nursery. Authoritarian people[72] grow up under the rule of dominating parents quick to use physical force as a means of imposing their will. 'It is a miracle that they ever survive the pressure and do not collapse under the burden of the commands laid upon them by their parents and teachers. That they in turn, and in equally cruel form, should give identical commands to their children is as natural as mastication or speech.'[73]

Jesus's – non-violent – attacks against rigidity and authoritarianism made him a true stumbling block to all forms of authority – parental, bureaucratic, educational, economic, and military, including the philosophical and theological ideologies that accompany and support them. That, by the preaching of obedience, and the ceaseless repetition of the saying 'Render therefore to Caesar the things that are Caesar's, and to God the things that are God's,'[74] the major Churches long ago have re-christened the real, disobedient Jesus is self-evident in the light of what has been said earlier on this point, and explains how it is that the official 'Church' Jesus is generally so popular, or is at least considered harmless, among policemen, judges, bankers, officials, politicians and other such representatives of power. But the real Jesus is reflected in a saying in which the house of the strong man is indeed entered with thoroughly subversive purpose: 'You know that those who are supposed to rule over the Gentiles lord it over them, and their great men exercise authority over them. But it shall not be so among you; but whoever would be great among you must be your servant, and whoever would be first among you must be slave of all.'[75]

That this call to a way of life free from hierarchical power structures, if it ever existed at all, did so only within Jesus's immediate circle, and (perhaps) in a few of the early Christian groups, will be discussed in the next chapter.

What matters in all this is that we can see the emergence of 'a rebellious expansion of human consciousness'[76] that is opposed to long-embedded attitudes of servility. And in proposing his own ideas Jesus had *not* cast out the devil with the power of Beelzebul, that is by grabbing power himself, flourishing swords, and plundering palaces. His method was to announce the imminent end of all power structures and chains of command, for which, instead, he holds a special place reserved – in hell.

Chapter 8
I call you friends

In the long course of church history no words of Jesus have been so frequently and so significantly repeated as: 'This is my body which is for you. Do this in remembrance of me.'[1]

Jesus's last meal with his disciples, though its significance is controversial, is numbered among the historically assured facts in our knowledge of Jesus's life. That Jesus established a sacramental rite in this meal is not clear and seems improbable.[2] It is very likely, however, that something so forceful issued from him at that time that the disciples wanted to remind and reassure themselves of it when the master was no longer with them. They therefore repeated that farewell meal time and again, as incidentally is credibly reported in the so-called Acts of the Apostles: 'And they devoted themselves to the apostles' teaching and fellowship, to the breaking of bread and the prayers. . . . And day by day, attending the temple together and breaking bread in their homes, they partook of food with glad and generous hearts.'[3]

By 'the breaking of bread' is meant the repetition of the last supper, and this took place informally in the people's homes, while the traditional religious services of these first Judeo-Christians continued to be held in the temple. The Acts of the Apostles describes the life of a relatively small group united by strong feelings of friendship. One is inevitably reminded of the equally small group of people with whom Jesus spent the days and nights of his public ministry. With these people Jesus cooked a few freshly caught fish, and slept beneath the stars or in whatever room was available. Though it was doubtless done without self-consciousness, such an intimately communal way of life is not easy to imagine. The extraordinarily short period of formation (in contrast to

Buddha and Mohammed who collected similar groups around them) needed by the group of disciples that gathered around Jesus was enough to lend it a high degree of stability and to withstand the crisis of the master's death. In this Jesus was successful, whereas, in the long run at least, all subsequent imitators have failed.

FOUR O'CLOCK IN THE AFTERNOON

Papyrus number 75, published in 1961 together with number 66 which had also only quite recently come to light, made available what was then the oldest Greek copy of John's gospel. It was dated between AD 175 and 225. But even older (about AD 130) was a papyrus fragment found some thirty-five years ago which contained a few lines from the eighteenth chapter of the same gospel.

Such results show with what zeal data is amassed that can in some way increase our knowledge of what happened in the first hundred years following the death of Jesus. In the present case it is a question of the date of composition of the fourth gospel. This gospel will be our particular concern in this chapter, for this gospel contains the largest number of clues concerning Jesus's relationship with his closest companions, the leitmotif being: 'Having loved his own who were in the world, he loved them to the end.'[4]

John's gospel,[5] the fourth and last in the New Testament, was written down by some unknown hand as the first century gave way to the second. It is the only gospel that constitutes an original literary treatment of what was known about Jesus, and it takes account of the oldest reports of Jesus's influence. Jesus did not speak as the fourth gospel would have him do so, ceremonially and like some distant God. But now and again, even in John's account, an idiomatic phrase appears, looking in the circumstances like a friendly snapshot in a family album otherwise filled with studio portraits. Thus, Peter says unceremoniously to his friends: ' "I am going fishing." They said to him, "We will go with you." . . . as day was breaking, Jesus stood on the beach . . . Jesus said to them, "Children, have you any fish?" '[6]

The same authentic touch is apparent in the story of how the

first disciples met up with Jesus on the banks of the Jordan[7] at the
time when John the Baptist held sway. What John then said about
Jesus, whom he saw coming towards him, led two of his, John's,
disciples to follow Jesus. Finally, Jesus turned round and said:
'What do you seek?' They answered him with a question: ' "Rabbi,
where are you staying?" He said to them, "Come and see." '

The text continues: 'They came and saw where he was staying;
and they stayed with him that day, for it was about the tenth hour.'
Someone noticed the time of day – four o'clock in the afternoon –
someone who was there at the time and in his subsequent narration
of the story thought this detail worthy of mention, until eventually
it was written down.

In this way, a group of men began to collect around Jesus. 'It
can be seen from the lives of the great founders that as a consequence of a decisive religious experience that they will have
interpreted as a "call", or at a particular age or period of their lives,
they begin to attract followers.'[8] Jesus apart, we find this with
Buddha, Mohammed, Confucius, Lao-tse, Zoroaster, Mani, and
Jina. Noticeable in each case, from the socio-psychological point
of view, is the masculine aspect. With the exception of Mohammed,
'they were without family sentiment. . . . But they had deep feeling
for their students or disciples. Their basic masculine attitude was
natural, not a product of will or principle.'[9] The gospels give this
close inner circle[10] different names: apostles, the twelve, the disciples.

The important qualification seems to have been that outlined
by Peter: those men 'who have accompanied us during all the time
that the Lord Jesus went in and out among us, beginning from the
baptism of John until the day when he was taken up from us'.[11]

It seems unlikely that we are speaking of more than twenty or
thirty men, even though Luke can refer to seventy disciples (or, if
the symbolism of numbers is taken into account, seventy-two – six
times twelve [Luke 10:1; variant readings]), and the Acts to 120;[12]
Paul on one occasion mentions as many as 500 brethren.[13]

According to Luke, there were also women with Jesus.[14] They
joined themselves to his following in Galilee and helped to look
after the group. There were also women beneath the cross. They

were there again at the empty tomb, and they assembled with Peter and the other disciples at Pentecost. Some of them are given names, such as Mary, from Magdala, a town notorious for its moral laxity. That Jesus had women in his following was a cause of great scandal at the time, and his provocative, gypsy-like commune attracted a good deal of contempt. He addressed his message to women, which was unheard of then, and as Mark tells us, he helped a woman suffering from a haemorrhage, an act that in those days could only have been considered downright indecent.[15] This sort of childish petulance followed Jesus everywhere. His group was very much a law unto itself as regards its social attitudes, and in its ready acceptance of women it was unique in the history of religion. Neither could it easily be said to have had a highly developed sense of so-called respectability.

SEE HOW HE LOVED HIM

Only in John's gospel do we learn that Jesus is capable of more personal relations: 'Now Jesus loved Martha and her sister and Lazarus.'[16]

That Jesus spent time in their house we are told by Luke.[17] But only the fourth gospel emphasizes Jesus's sympathy for Lazarus.[18] It tells us that Jesus wept for his dead friend and that the guests who were present commented: 'See how he loved him!'

The fourth gospel is also the only one to make reference to the disciple whom Jesus loved.[19] It is probable that this is a reference to John himself, that is, the man who gave the gospel its name. Only in John's gospel does Jesus call his disciples his friends: 'No longer do I call you servants, for the servant does not know what his master is doing; but I have called you friends, for all that I have heard from my Father I have made known to you.'[20]

In a famous passage in his *Phenomenology of Mind*,[21] Hegel presented lordship and bondage as two opposed forms of consciousness – on the one hand the independent form of it in the master, on the other its dependent manifestation in the bondsman. If this analysis is relevant here, then according to the fourth gospel

Jesus wanted to dissolve this opposition between his own dominant consciousness and the subject consciousness of his disciples. But this does not mean to say that he wished to lose his own distinct and unmistakable identity: 'You call me Teacher and Lord; and you are right, for so I am. If I then, your Lord and Teacher, have washed your feet, you also ought to wash one another's feet. For I have given you an example, that you also should do as I have done to you.'[22]

In the fourth gospel's account of the last supper (from which this passage comes) we see Jesus choosing a humbling act so as to demonstrate to his disciples what he has in mind; one after the other, he washes their dirty feet – in other words, he does the work of a slave.[23] The speechless bewilderment thereby engendered prepares the company for a possible appreciation of his intention, which he then goes on to outline. In doing so, Jesus reduces his own leadership role within the group, though of course he does not actually surrender it. What he seeks is a non-authoritarian relationship; he wants to rid his disciples of the notion of submission, and of the related concepts of rank and place on the hierarchical ladder; each should serve the other.

What Jesus is preaching is known as *agape*, a word seldom found in other writings of those days, and yet a common one in the New Testament. The nearest English equivalent of the word is 'love'.

According to the fourth gospel, this is not an attitude of love for mankind generally, expressed in some abstract way, but is one that refers specifically to the (small) group: 'Greater love has no man than this, that a man lay down his life for his friends.'[24]

The reader searches in vain for anything in John's gospel about founding a church, baptizing people, a world mission, and a hierarchy of office in a yet-to-be-created major religious complex. Even the kingdom of God, so important for Jesus, features here as something quite lowly and free from the notion of kingship.

'This living harmony among men, and their communion with God, is what Jesus calls the kingdom of God. Jesus took the word "kingdom" from the Hebrew, and it is a word that introduces something quite alien into the expression of the divine union of mankind, in as far as it describes only a unity built on direct rule, on the force exerted by one stranger over another, a force that must be kept out of the beauty and the divine life of a pure human covenant.'[25] The fourth gospel was successful in achieving this separation for even the corresponding expression (*basileia tou theou*=kingdom of God) occurs only once,[26] and then with an altered meaning – that is, without the occurrence of cosmic destruction and re-formation.

Again, we can quote the young Hegel, who as a student with Hölderlin and Schelling in a Tübingen seminary dreamed of a new form of Christianity: 'A circle of love, of sentiment, whose members have surrendered all special rights in respect of one another and are united only through faith and hope held in common, and whose pleasure and joy lies only in this pure harmony of love, such would be a small kingdom of God.'

But all the Johannine Jesus asks is, 'that you love one another as I have loved you'.[27]

What is astonishing about these words is that they are found of all places in a gospel that in its solemn prologue and elsewhere presents Jesus as a figure of divine light descending from on high – a gospel, in short, that is anything but everyday in its approach. This at least suggests the possibility that between the lines there speaks one whose memory of the true Jesus is strong enough to hold its own against all the divine pomp with which the writer surrounds Jesus.

HIS OWN PEOPLE RECEIVED HIM NOT

'Jesus's fate was not quite that of his community; as it consisted of various people thrown together but all living apart from the world, each member was able to find several like-minded companions. They stuck together and were able to hold themselves remote from the world at large, and as this meant that contact and therefore friction was reduced, they were accordingly less attracted by the world and spent less of their time in the purely negative occupation of defence. This must have increased their desire for a positive way of life, for there is neither pleasure nor beauty in a community life based on negative principles.'[28]

Jesus in bad company

This analysis is based on what we know of the earliest Christian community in Jerusalem, information that comes to us from the Acts of the Apostles written by Luke (sometime soon after AD 70): 'Now the company of those who believed were of one heart and soul, and no one said that any of the things which he possessed was his own, but they had everything in common. . . . for as many as were possessors of lands or houses sold them, and brought the proceeds of what was sold and laid it at the apostles' feet; and distribution was made to each as any had need . . .' and they had 'favour with all the people'.[29]

Interesting in this report from the socio-psychological point of view is not so much the much-discussed communism of love practised by the first Christians, as the inference that there were no tensions between this (minority) group and their social environment. It all sounds very peaceable. The Christians come across as a happy crowd, guileless, at peace with the world, wanting no revenge, daily attracting new members.

Neither do the difficulties with the police that were soon to begin much affect this situation, at least not at first. One hears of trials, and of the temporary imprisonment of the apostles. On one of these occasions, when up before the high priest, Peter showed that he had no intention of concealing his loyalties: 'We must obey God rather than men.'[30]

But, to start with, all seems to go well. The apostles are free to travel where they will and they take advantage of this to spread their influence, even after Stephen had been stoned and a certain Saul had emerged as a trouble-shooter. Later, after he had been exposed to the light of heaven while on his way to Damascus, this Saul became Paul, an ardent representative of Jesus.[31] Once again, the Christians in Palestine had their liberty: 'So the church throughout all Judea and Galilee and Samaria had peace and was built up; and walking in the fear of the Lord and in the comfort of the Holy Spirit it was multiplied.'[32]

That is the Acts of the Apostles' verdict on what was happening in Jesus's own country during the first decade of Christianity. On the domestic political front, these Jesus groups appear to have been without significance. The Jewish historian Flavius Josephus, who lived in the second half of the first century, mentioned neither Jesus nor the Christians in his extensive historical writings (the one passage in which such reference is made is of disputed validity).

The believers in the land of the Jews gave no trouble; they observed the Torah and avoided disputes; Jesus came for Israel's sake, wishing to bring his people the forgiveness of sins. God gave him his blessing, and he will come again as the Messiah so as to renew the earth.[33]

This picture of the development of the first Christian groups during the first ten years of their existence within Palestine can be tested by subjecting it to our knowledge of social psychology, or more precisely group dynamics. According to the first law, as adumbrated by G. C. Homans, the increase in the frequency of contacts between two or more persons is linked with an increase in the feelings of sympathy that exist between them.[34]

And further: An increase in the interior contacts (contacts between the members of a group) leads to a diminution of outward contacts (contacts between members of a group and its environment). Thus, Homans's second law. But it takes account of yet another factor, and that is the increase in the distaste on the part of the group for those outside the group. But we have not yet come across this in our discussion of how things were among the first Christians. Perhaps the problem really didn't arise until after the first years of fresh innocence.

It is certain that the miraculous peace of the first years didn't last very long; one only has to read the first three gospels to discover that. As we have seen, much of what they contain has little to do with the actions and words of the true Jesus, but is to be attributed to accounts of his life and message initiated by these early Christian groups. Thus, for instance, much of what the gospels say about the bitter dispute between Jesus and the Pharisees comes from these groups. This alone is enough to demonstrate that tension did exist between Palestine's Christian communities and their environment.

But when we turn to the fourth gospel we see that the brotherly love has gone and that irritability is evident as early as the famous prologue where the in-group stands in sharp contrast to those outside: 'We have beheld his glory. . . . And from his fullness have we all received'[35] – thus the believers in Jesus.

But of those outside, the rest of mankind, we read: 'Yet the world knew him not. He came to his own home, and his own people received him not.'

'He' – that, of course, means Jesus. 'His own people' – those are the Jews. The problem begins with the puzzling unbelief of the Jews. Seventy-one times, the fourth gospel refers quite simply to 'the Jews', whereas the other three gospels only use the expression sixteen times between them, showing instead a preference for the use of specific group names (Pharisees, scribes, the elders, etc.).

Additionally, the fourth gospel tends towards a strong ideological polarization which expresses itself among other ways through contrasts: Light – Darkness, Truth – Lies, Spirit – Flesh (all three used in common with the Qumran literature); and then, Death – Life, Below – Above, Earthly – Heavenly, God – World, Freedom – Servitude.

Black/white thinking of this type is an accepted characteristic of a well-integrated group with strong internal emotional connections – to which in this case minority status must also be added. The positive side of the contrasting pairs listed above represents the self-evaluation of the in-group, the negative pole in each case being reserved for their opponents outside the group.

Given this sort of background, one can see how it is that in the fourth gospel when it comes to the crunch even Jesus is only permitted to pray for the group: 'I am not praying for the world but for those whom thou hast given me.'[36]

'Love is not recommended, unless it be in very small groups.'[37] According to what has just been said even this modest conclusion cannot be fully accepted – when love of neighbour also means love for one's enemies. About seventy years elapsed between the death of Jesus and the appearance of John's gospel; not even for as long as this could Jesus's message of love endure, at least not in an ethical form that can be found convincing today.

Chapter 9
Translation difficulties

To date, most of what has been written about Jesus has been written in Greek, Latin, Italian, Spanish, French, English, and German. Important theological and philosophical works of the Christian millennium between the barbarian invasions and the discovery of America, learned discussions from the post-Christian era between Luther and Hitler – nearly all are the fruits of the Indo-European system of speech, thought, and literary composition.

'Thought is formed by grammar.'[1] The Chinese, Tibetans, Turks, and Africans do not merely speak differently from us, but have a style of thought that is fashioned in a quite different way. The idiom of Jesus was Semitic – one that does not belong to the Indo-European group of languages. The gospels contain only the smallest handful of words[2] directly attributable to Jesus – everything else was at once paraphrased and adapted.

Some insight into the influence of grammar on thought can be gained through the findings of the pertinent science, which, under the name of linguistics, owes much of its initial impetus to the work of Edward Sapir (d. 1939). Today this area of research is developing strongly, and it has important implications and applications in the fields of social psychology, cultural anthropology, logic, and linguistic philosophy.

The civilizing triumphal progress of Indo-European speech and thought is now a global fact, though this should not necessarily lead us to see our system of grammar as the only one; there are other ways of doing things, as we may perhaps discover from China and Japan within the foreseeable future.

Jesus in bad company

The thoughts we have about Jesus are dependent on the language we speak and this means that we are not entitled to consider them definitive. In a different set of linguistic circumstances, different things could be thought about Jesus, things that because of the limitations of our own grammatical system would never occur to us.

In moments when thought has no language, as for instance in the ecstasy of the mystics, it can develop notions about Jesus independent of the various grammatical systems. It is not impossible that such views would differ fundamentally from the conventional conception of Jesus. Yet we see from a study of mystics from radically differing cultures that they all suffer from the difficulty of clothing their thoughts in a comprehensible linguistic form. Mysticism lacks a grammar and as a result its most decisive experiences remain incommunicable.

Perpaps the poet mediates between mysticism and ordinary speech. He is, in any event, more difficult to translate than a newspaper report. Perhaps a good poet is less dependent on grammar than the rest of us in that he develops new linguistic forms and to that extent new thought forms.

What I am getting at is the wisdom, when reflecting about Jesus, of giving a thought to the instruments we use in the process; in other words the nouns and verbs and their combination into sentences according to certain rules. Such an exercise might then prove useful when language is abused, for it will help to bring to our attention something that otherwise comes to us as easily as breathing: our habits of speech. Normally, we pay no attention to them at all, and because we pay them no attention we think them ideal.

Breathing difficulties direct the attention to one's breathing, a process that otherwise happens completely of itself. Language difficulties can cause us to take note of language. In Jesus's case, language difficulties are easy to find when one thinks of the obscurity of many theological utterances, or the ceremonial vacuity of official ecclesiastical statements. Most people seem to have language difficulties when they come to speak about

Jesus; so often they produce fundamentally childish formulas.

But people tend to cling on to the various formulas, and debates about some of them fill whole books. Whether or not Jesus was God's son. Whether or not he walked on the waters. Whether or not he is risen from the dead. Whether or not Joseph is his real father.

If this book lacks discussion of subjects that perhaps many would consider essential, it does so consciously. What still remains to be said might be thought of as a grammatical exercise, as therapy for a case of linguistic cramp, written with Jesus as starting-point, looking at him as far as he can be seen until further notice.

It would be pleasing if in the process at least a few people were released from the burden of confusing the true Jesus with the picture of him that emerges from the language and thought forms that have accumulated around him in the course of time.

Chapter 10

The circumstance of place

He who has found no proper place in society is looked upon with distrust. Stateless people, for example; people who have no fixed address or regular income. A man who doesn't know where he belongs arouses suspicion, and not only from official quarters; one simply doesn't trust him out of sight; he is not a dependable person. In contrast, if a man is well placed socially, and has a good job, then one knows where one stands. The young man the girl brought home is in the living room: they want to see if he'll do as an eventual husband.

We all carry our position finders around with us; they form a part of our character, and what is left when they are removed may in many cases seem like an empty container into which various things have been poured, things natural to us and things acquired. That young man in the living room is fortunate if he is of good family and if there is money around. A mark is made in his favour. To struggle against the question of one's origins is difficult, as Jesus himself experienced: 'Can anything good come out of Nazareth?' A man may feel he has something to be ashamed of – perhaps he is illegitimate, or has a father in prison; so he has to watch out in case he betrays himself.

Alcoholics, criminals, prostitutes, the mentally disturbed, the neglected, the socially maladjusted, the work-shy, the neurotics – they all suffer from unfavourable origins, their mother didn't love them, five children in one bed; nothing good comes of such situations.

Topos is approximately the Greek equivalent for place, and an *atopotatos*[1] is one who has no proper place in society. Socrates was thus described by his fellow citizens in Athens. No one really knew where to pigeon-hole him. He was looked upon as an eccentric.

That an outsider should have such an enduring influence must seem strange to the socio-geographical way of thought. There's a man who can't be placed and yet who continues to exert an influence long after his death.

Everything has its proper place, and only when it's seen to be in it do we feel at home, only then does our environment constitute an area in which we feel safe, even on waking in the morning. It is a strange feeling to wake up in a strange bed, not quite knowing where one is. But things quickly sort themselves out; in a fraction of a second the overloaded brain copes with the fresh information, we recall where we are and the foreseeable events of the coming day can be looked in the eye. In short, we're back in our own place.

One could argue that Jesus has called us to a life of minimal security. His own social geography was hardly exemplary, and what he thought as he woke up each morning would be worth consideration. But one would need a lot of imagination and it is exactly that quality that tends to languish the deeper our particular rut becomes.

When it comes to getting a job, considerable importance attaches to what one knows, what schools one attended, what university, and so on. A *curriculum vitae* written for this purpose is presented in a sort of telegraphese and is laid out so as to lead directly to what at each turn really matters in life. The reader is supposed to gain a clear picture of the applicant's social position. What he needs is the right man for the right job, and if first impressions are favourable, then more subtle means can be employed to discover more.

Some positions call for a high degree of dependability, which means predictability of behaviour. What matters here is the applicant's disposition, his political attitudes, his way of looking at life. References are required; the candidate is subjected to intensive investigation. Conducting an investigation at this level is a specialized job. Sometimes things go wrong, as when a man conceals his true attitudes, or in fact has none and so merely simulates those required of him. Socrates, for example, had no particular point of view other than his own desire to enquire after truth, and this caused him to be called a corrupter of youth.

Judging by the official Jesus figure put out by the Churches, it would appear that he had a particular way of looking at life and the world. It would appear that he had the correct and ready answer to every question, as though his teaching contained an ordered system clarifying every aspect of life. That such a picture of Jesus could develop is not entirely the fault of the clerical element in the official interpretation of his life and work, but is also a consequence of the desire for order and for pigeon-holing; Jesus is allotted his place, is called the Son of God, founder of a religion, who sits at the right hand of God. We have moulded him to our needs so as to make him readily recognizable, someone we can depend upon, who made a career for himself and achieved something.

The truth is that Jesus was not at all reliable. He roused people's anger and provoked unrest, was a stumbling block and a cause of scandal. He escapes every attempt to pigeon-hole him. He is severe when one might expect him to be mild, yielding where one might expect him to be decisive. He prayed in the temple and yet called for its destruction, upset his own family and then included close relatives in the circle of his disciples. And everywhere he met the question: Who are you? How do we place you? Are you the Messiah? Are you the prophet? Will you restore the kingdom of Israel? In whose authority do you act?

Jesus side-stepped all such questions, snapped his fingers at red tape, enjoyed his food and drink where asceticism was expected of him, acknowledged a following but distributed no weapons, spoke of the end of the world but did not forget the priorities of the daily round.

His frequent change of position is purposeless rather than intended. His rootlessness is not part of a programme. He wants to change thought, not direct it along new lines that would simply become another rut.

'Jesus the King of the Jews': even the notice pinned to the cross[2] was an appalling embarrassment. It is not surprising that they finally nailed him there: at least he'd make no more trouble.

The navigator guides the ship safely across the ocean. He determines her position at any given moment with the help of a range of instruments. The conscience may be likened to such an instrument. It tells us if we are still on the right road, or if we have deviated from it. Jesus deviated from the right road. Something or other was wrong with his conscience. It remains to be noted that Jesus was not, alas, a particularly conscientious person.

A conscientious person navigates well, has a nose for the right direction, for where one has come from and where one is heading for; in other words, for the circumstance of place. Conscience is fashioned differently according to the society in which it operates. What is permitted in one place is forbidden in another. But whatever the case, a man has to be able to navigate. It is a process in which the individual behaves like a pedestrian on a busy pavement – the nature and speed of his own movements is in large part determined by the movements of others.

A conscientious person maintains his own position by respecting that of others. He plays his radio so that it is not heard through the wall. He does as he would be done by.

That is morality's so-called golden rule. It appears to have made a greater impression in the animal kingdom than among men. For though animals fight for position, they do not have wars. The attitude that conscientious navigation is sufficient hasn't yet got us very far. It is also conscientious to construct bomb shelters.

By avoiding status seeking and the rat race Jesus is contributing to the fullness of human nature, attacking that part of the brain that produces feelings of aggression. But so far he hasn't had much success. One does not make his intentions one's own by taking note of them but by putting them into effect; for the behaviour patterns one is trying to root out are deeply ingrained, reaching back to the time when we were still swinging from trees, cowering before the dominant member of the group.

To be imprisoned can provide good practice in what it was that Jesus stood for. Mark refers to the likelihood of it happening: 'For they will deliver you up to councils.'[3]

When incarcerated, one's social geography is stood on its head; a disagreeable experience. The law is an excellent thing as long as one has nothing to do with it. But in prison one is quite definitely in the wrong place and they make sure that you know it. Paul learned all about it: '. . . with far greater labours, far more imprisonments, with countless beatings, and often near death',[4] '. . . destitute, afflicted, ill-treated'.[5] In prison, should he happen to be there, much can be learned about Jesus by one who would follow him. Such a one anyway belongs among the convicts – though not, of course, for the same reason as the common criminal.

Jesus's follower should rejoice as he hears the key turn in the lock: 'Blessed are you when men revile you and persecute you and utter all kinds of evil against you falsely on my account.'[6]

Another exercise for the student of Jesus is the reversal of his social direction. The place our journey leads to lies down below and not up there with the rich: property and good breeding all lead upwards, as is right and proper.

Augustine compared love with the (specific) weight of the body: 'In my case, love is the weight by which I act. . . . A body inclines by its own weight towards the place that is fitting for it.'[7] The man who loves has a new specific weight, strives to attain something other than social position; his attitude to man and things undergoes a reversal, his attention and interest is aroused precisely at the point at which conventional attitudes fail: he notices what others pass by. Romeo and Juliet are a case in point: they are attracted to one another and pay no heed to the deadly enmity of their two families. Their attitude could hardly be less practical. Two students, a girl and a boy, leave home together. Something of that sort is often in the papers. The police are called in. Jesus winks at them.

sleeping in the open in Umbria can be extremely cold. But Bernardo tried it. Practice makes perfect, and everything else will take care of itself.

There have also been collective attempts to depart from the traditional social gamut. Not for a long time with any success, but always on Christian ground, in other words with Jesus in the background. The notion that the world will one day disappear and thereafter return again in a totally new form is foreign to Africans and Asians. Thoughts of this kind come from the Near East.

The world is evil. We want another, better one. That's where the revolution begins. But in taking up arms the revolutionary attends only to man-made circumstances, raising his eyes no higher. For even the maddest fanatic knows that you can't drink all the water in the sea.

It was not Jesus who established hope in the Last Day: it existed before his time. He fostered it in his way, and also compromised with it, like all his predecessors and successors up to and including the Adventists – who have often had to push forward their date for the end of the world.

Mao Tse-tung did not need Jesus on his Long March. It is both presumptuous and superfluous to build Jesus up into the father of all revolutionaries. From Spartacus to Castro rebellions and uprisings have taken place without him. Jesus has not always played part in the two-thousand-year-old tradition of revolt. And rebels have not always chosen Jesus as their patron; those in Naples chose t Januarius and in Palermo they appointed St Rosalia.[12]

Ideologues of every type have offered the historical Jesus fierce resistance. Fundamentally, they are not in the least interested in him, but just use him to suit their own ends. Many an army has done battle in the name of Jesus, and done it against another army fighting in the same name. But this tells us nothing about Jesus. He is not sympathetic to programmes, he's not a joiner, is neither Catholic, Jewish, nor Communist. Feelings of belonging lead once again to the social climb, to fixed points, to hardening of attitudes.

Jesus frustrates the social compass and builds a magn
his own. Anyone who allows himself to be diverted
finds himself in wonderland. Anyone who looks for ar
pearl of great price that Jesus mentioned in the parabl
everything in order to own it, moves mountains,[9] an
will be with me in Paradise'.[10]

Hansel and Gretel are standing by the side of th
They want to go to Italy. Their parents are beside the
worry. But the children are recaptured. Perhaps, tho
with the outcome, the newspaper reader feels a ti
'Unless you turn and become like children, you will n
kingdom of heaven.'[11] One could well envy the two tr
everything and spend a few days under the sun. But
that get one? The money won't last for ever and th
next meal to think of. Once again, Jesus has lost out
are extremely small. They lie in the weak pull of envy
then seizes the well-to-do as they reflect upon s
enjoyable escapade.

Here is a passage from the so-called *fioretti*, the collec
about Francis of Assisi: As St Francis still wen
clothes of people of the world, many people thoug
fool. He had to put up with ceaseless derision fr
strangers alike. But he, patient and serene, let it all
like one deaf and dumb. Then a man called Bernar
most noble, the most wealthy, and the most wis
town, began to think differently and to point out
Francis's rejection of the world, the greatness
amidst mortifications, and the strength of his pati
them. . . . What made the rich man begin to rethi
He was well placed socially and had plenty of pre
wrong?

What caused him finally to drop everything a
Francis? His friends shook their heads. They p
indoors.

The text speaks of 'serenity'. Perhaps Bernar
new level of happiness. But if so, then on an emp

Even in the Roman circus the factions had their blues and greens.

Nevertheless Jesus does sometimes take one side rather than another, though it's not always easy at any given moment to tell which side. We would not find him in Hitler's ranks, although one might wonder why, for there was faith there too, and the reign of a thousand years[13] outlined in Revelation beckoned.

Does Jesus share the passive patience of those who, remote from the world, await its end? Or is he numbered among the active and full of hope who want to get something done here and now, whether a farming project or the overthrow of a régime? Where does he seek solidarity – with the farmer or the industrial worker, the coloured people or the whites, the bourgeois or the intellectuals? Or with the so-called homeless and uprooted? Does he shout with those who encourage the class struggle, or is he concerned rather to even out existing social contrasts? Does he hold with the Black Panther movement, or General Franco, or Gandhi, or Martin Luther King, or the Pope? Does he prefer atheists to pious people? Are his actions premeditated or are they not? Is he a loner or does he prefer crowds?

Where is Jesus?

Again the circumstance of place, but now ethically something that must be answered; Jesus must make his viewpoint known; we want to force him to do so. If he says nothing, then we're perfectly entitled to ignore him. If he runs away when the crunch comes, then he vanishes from history. Whoever, speaking of Jesus, perpetually says this but also that, will, as is well known, be spat out, for meanwhile the world goes round.

Jesus is with the children who run away from home. He is with prisoners and with the condemned. Always with the poor. Never with the rich. Always with the dissatisfied, avoiding those who have enough. He is not with the preservers of the *status quo*; they can get along without him.

Jesus sides with the weak. He feels committed to those who are angry. He doesn't attend inaugural meetings.

He's seldom seen in churches, for there he's worshipped anyway. He dresses unobtrusively and never ever wears a uniform.

And he never stays anywhere for long.

He wasn't in the world for very long. He's difficult to imagine as a middle-aged man. Therein lies his weakness and his strength.

His weakness: He is inimitable. He lived too short a time to be otherwise, said too little that was unambiguous, too often asked the impossible.

His strength: He is not overtaxed and so does not wear himself out; does not tie himself down, works indirectly, not programmatically, and never dogmatically. One cannot discern his true significance by a theoretical approach, only through actual practice.

Whoever feels attracted by Jesus cannot adequately explain why. He must be prepared to be always correcting his image of Jesus, for he will never exhaust what there is to know. Jesus is full of surprises. Tomorrow will look after itself.

Resignation, a developed sense of reality, and submission to fate come of themselves as one advances in age. But one who doesn't know where he can lay his head can learn a lot from Jesus.

In a Lisbon seminary a few years ago a leaflet appeared in the form of a police notice. Whoever wrote it was on to a very different Jesus: one whose social place is that of a Wanted Person:

Relevant information is requested that might lead to the arrest of Jesus Christ accused of seduction, anarchistic tendencies and conspiring against the State.

Special characteristics: scars on hands and feet.

Alleged profession: carpenter.

Nationality: Jewish.

Aliases: Son of Man, Prince of Peace, Light of the World.

No fixed address.

The wanted man preaches the equality and freedom of all people, represents Utopian ideas and must be described as a dangerous agitator. Members of the public are asked to report any relevant information to their nearest police station.

Chapter 11
The circumstance of time

The party's over, the game is through. Jesus is on the cross, still alive, but soon to die. The whole process is said to have lasted three hours. Then they all went home. Never, until today, has a dénouement been accompanied by such profound and lengthy attentiveness. It is not the moment of death that is here of interest. One does not experience death. But the process itself. The endgame.

Decay is everywhere. One only has to open one's eyes to see it. Women scour the mirror for the lines of age. Teeth are filled. Childhood illnesses are numerous, sometimes fatal. Even at thirty a man can suffer from blood pressure troubles. Doctors, opticians, and dispensing chemists need fear no economic recession; their trade is assured. Minor cuts, too, are unpleasant, and sometimes a leg has to be amputated. A man who suffers from cancer of the throat is particularly unfortunate. He has to be fed through a tube in his throat, and cannot leave his bed. Cleaning one's teeth, and washing, are ways of protecting health, and we go on holiday to recuperate and to renew our strength. Mineral waters contain many useful ingredients. Smoke too much and we outrage our own body. Exercise keeps us young and fresh, but damage can result if it's overdone.

The washing-up has to be done; shoes have to be cleaned. The vacuum cleaner helps the housewife with her housework. There's always dust. Cleansing and washing agents help to preserve what we have; preservatives also form a major branch of the food industry – fruit, vegetables, fish, and meat are tinned, otherwise they would rot. Putting them in tins keeps decay temporarily at bay.

Buildings, streets, and machines come in good, fair, and bad condition; they're always needing repair, restoration, renewal. Venice is sinking into the sea and will continue to do so unless a huge rescue programme is launched. The conservation of what exists can be expressed as a cost; the maintenance of plant and machinery must be taken into account in the budget.

Fashion has to keep the market supplied with novelties, and not just in clothes and jewellery. Ideas, writers, trends, get used up like winter coats. There is always something else just round the corner; that something was on the way out attracts less attention – room has to be made for what is coming; time has run out for the actor, indeed one hasn't heard anything of him for ages. A pity, really.

But if something does manage to hang on for a longer period, it gains greatly in respect, is called classical and is said to be here to stay. Time is powerless before the Venus de Milo and the Mona Lisa.

State and family survive the individual. One speaks of institutions. They must be left alone. They've kept themselves intact and though sometimes their form has changed they've always been around.

Whatever successfully withstands the circumstance of time we call dependable. A connection with a bank, a relationship between two people.

Something that could be quite different this time tomorrow is called unreliable. One protects oneself against such things. Desertion is severely punished. One must play the game and play it straight.

Reactions to transience and decay differ. The housewife reacts bravely and practically; sufficient unto the day is the evil thereof. Others become moody; for them the whole world grows old; and at the end of it all is entropy. Others exploit the moment, pluck the rose before the bloom fades. Or, faced with life's changing fortunes, a man may seek peace of mind, and cultivate a stoical and sceptical disengagement; mystics and cynics withdraw into themselves; both say all is 'vanity',[1] though each means something different.

We should have a look at the figure of the founder, precisely because Jesus wasn't one. Romulus and Remus set out to start something, to initiate something that would last. Laying the foundation stone, the charter of foundation, on this rock I will build my church,[2] eternal Rome. The founder in spite of the circumstance of time, building for eternity; his works will survive him, his name will live for ever written in the most enduring material, incised in stone; commemorative monuments are erected to him. In this way, security measures are taken against the circumstance of time, against decay and transience. As ideal figure at least, the founder is not unaware of settling dust and omnipresent rust, looks as far into the future as possible, calculates the foreseeable signs of wear and tear in his undertaking, plans for centuries in advance.

The founding element still survives in associations and the like, though they're not nearly so demanding. But memorial days are celebrated: look, we've been around for sixty years, and the jubilee marks a small triumph against the progress of decay. Even when a family house is being built, care is taken to ensure that the building will still be serviceable for the grandchildren.

The founder has to overcome resistance, and the stronger the resistance the more extensive his plans. What is already there puts up a fight against new foundations, feels threatened, and quite rightly, because the founder has branded it decayed, out of date. In vain did the Indians fight against the white settlers; the times were against them; let's get rid of them; the only good Indian is a dead one.

The successful revolutionary becomes a founder, his negative will to destroy turning into a positive will to rebuild. We shall build a new world. Successful foundations are self-centred, signify progress, distance themselves from their predecessors, call them old. The Christians called the Torah the Old Testament, as opposed to their own new one. The time before the French Revolution is called the *ancien régime*.

Sometimes what is old is brought back into service, exhumed;

then one speaks of Renaissance, Restoration, Reformation; the past had merely simulated death; now it lives afresh; Aristotle is once again modern, the once cursed nobility returns to France.

It is doubtful that one can learn from history. Something or other is proceeding on its way. People sometimes say that history is a circular movement spread over immensely long periods of time, the ceaseless return of the same. But this point of view has yet to be confirmed. Such considerations are of minor importance to the founder. In him one speaks rather of the primacy of will. Alexander the Great just upped and went.

Rien ne va plus, the roulette wheel spins; it's Jesus's last chance – and Paul's too: 'The form of this world is passing away.'[3] Everything is moving towards its end. Modern theologians call this eschatology, hiding behind an unfamiliar word that none but they understands.

Rien ne va plus: The basic mood of the end of the world makes any sort of foundation irrelevant; the most one could accept would be something entirely provisional. 'Hereafter you will see the Son of man . . . coming on the clouds of heaven.'[4]

At once we hear an objection from a historian: It was customary in those days to think in terms of the end of the world and the corresponding linguistic imagery was widespread. Jesus was in no way original in these references.

Even so, it remains puzzling that all the other fanatics of those days and later, for instance those that lived towards the end of the Middle Ages, are long forgotten and now exist only in history books. But Jesus is not so easily got rid of, and this in spite of the postponed end.

'Finished, it's finished, nearly finished, it must be nearly finished.' Samuel Beckett[5] writes economically; the man who is dying can only drag himself from one moment to the next. Death could come at any moment. But it doesn't *have* to. The end of the world is at the threshold but there is time between it and the living; the end could come at any moment while not having to come at any *particular* moment, and so we wait from moment to moment.

The size of the hour-glass is not known, nor how much sand has already slipped through the funnel.

'It must be nearly finished': that's what the waiting man says as he feels the tension of the moment. In reality one doesn't wait from moment to moment for the beloved; one just looks now and again to see what the time is, thinking of something different in the intervals. Hearing some noise or other, one says to oneself: perhaps that's her.

Looked at in this way death, which is bound to come, and the girl friend who arrived on time anyway, both come as surprises. The surprise lies in the fact that death, the woman, the end of the world, arrive in this particular second, tenth, hundredth, thousandth of a second, not the very smallest unit of time earlier or later.

One does, of course, have to wait while something is coming to an end. And it is from the tension it produces that we gain some inkling of what is meant by time.

A wide range of words has been used to describe Jesus's relationship to the world: indifference, opposition, a relationship of tension, rejection, enmity, questioning; a revolutionary way of thought, rebellion, thinking in terms of catastrophes.

They all have one thing in common: Jesus was not at all happy about the shape of things: in tribe and family, religion, class and social distinctions, the owning of goods, power structures, education.

He saw all these things within the process of ending and so he issued the call to awareness, waiting,[6] in relation to the circumstance of time, to the moments in which we hear the ticking of the clocks. There is no need to get rid of reality, for it already contains the worm of decay. What we have to watch out for is each moment in the cosmic endgame, for each moment could bring the end. Perhaps *this* is the moment.

This is an attitude of observance; the stuff our world is made of is subjected to continuous examination for wear and tear. We are living in mankind's last days.

The sun is shining. But for how much longer? A cheque is cashed, soldiers march: for how much longer? Marriages, births, deaths, growth rates, government crises: for how much longer? I am hungry; I need to relieve myself. For how much longer?

If all is given up to decay then dejection can set in, an inability to enjoy anything. But Jesus's preaching was not melancholy. Autumn and winter were not preferred as backgrounds to his message.

Indeed, more often than not the gospels mention summer[7] and the coming harvest. Or a woman in childbirth.[8] The accent is on the careful observation of life in process; something is always pursuing its appropriate course,[9] the corn ripens, the pains become stronger.

It is natural to man to experience decay and decline as negative things; no one relishes a broken heart. As a result, all endings are illuminated with a pale light; death nods from afar. This explains how the cliché comes into being: the Roman Empire is fallen, the Habsburg Dynasty is vanished, the British Empire is gone. All of which is perfectly true if one considers the underlying political criteria important. Even as a book title, *Decline of the West*[10] invites sympathy, regret, horror.

But such gloomy feelings are not necessarily warranted; endings can also be evaluated positively: perhaps there is something better to come.

According to John's gospel, Jesus's last words were: 'It is finished.'[11]

From this point of view – and one is inclined to share it – the ending is given a significance that is no longer merely passive. Death, then, means: being ready. Bringing something to an end, completion, fulfilment.

Remarkable here is that this ending takes place in a situation in which nothing more can be done. Hands and feet are nailed to the cross, while sharp pains make it impossible to say very much. So one might reasonably expect passivity to dominate; and yet Jesus is actively finishing something. So that passivity and activity are no longer alternatives, they have no ultimate value as points of orientation.

If, as we are doing here, we say that Jesus's death had an exemplary value with regard to our own lives, then we shan't get very far with a further aid to orientation of a conceptual nature, namely that contained in the negative-positive contrast. For there can be no doubt but that Jesus's death was negative enough; and yet the party ended positively. Jesus had the last word; he won.

The crucifix (in use since AD 400) has remained the most common, the most enduring, and also the most popular representation of Jesus. It preserves either the end (eyes shut) or the process of ending (eyes open). It is noteworthy that iconographically no one has been able to deify Jesus crucified. With the end of the Romanesque period in art the crown and royal mantle vanish. Something that has been clung to so tenaciously, something so contrary to the heavenly kingdom, and in the midst of the cult of splendour, demands attention.

The crucifix is not only used as something to hold up before the dying: the healthy look at it as well. Jesus's way of death is inseparable from his way of life, which in turn was clearly enough determined by his end.

Or, to be more precise, by bearing in mind the end to come – for reference to the approaching end is as integral a part of Jesus as his social rootlessness, a condition that now becomes easier to understand, for one sees an object in it: we cannot place Jesus socially because family, religion, property, class, and the apparatus of power are to him all transient; they are signs of the end.

That the talk of an imminently expected end was illusory gives Jesus's own approach to his death a tension which, were it not there, would detract from his invitation to sit up and take note. Jesus's mistake with regard to the imminent end is indispensable to our understanding of his purpose. One should not excuse the mistake or explain it away, as it is an integral feature of his message; the habitual reflection on the end as an attitude to life is in ceaseless compromise with continuing reality.

For the sun is still shining, people still get married, study, work; people are still tortured; people still think about things. The world spins onward, progress is made, we weep, laugh, breathe, no gain without pain, no bricks without straw; youth must have its ideals – they can all be shed later.

One has to ask if identification with Jesus achieves anything that it is difficult to achieve in any other way. He is certainly still an effective and appealing figure for the masses, not just in books and churches for the individual; he preaches wordlessly to many. He is able to inspire in man the will to improve himself as a species.

But what does Jesus offer with regard to the circumstance of time?

He dissolves the cramped preservation of what exists.

He plays along when something intolerable is being liquidated. He sharpens our powers of observation in the assessment of age and decay.

He keeps us on the *qui vive*; he awakens sleeping disciples.

He thwarts the fear of death.

He does not yield to the inevitable.

But he knows when to stop, how to finish something, to find a conclusion. He holds on to nothing, not even himself.

For as long as men fight against the end, Jesus will have something to say. For as long as love fights against the end by designating its object through possessive pronouns, Jesus can step in as a corrective. For as long as there is war in which what was formerly preserved with such care can be destroyed at a stroke, Jesus retains his licence as saviour. For as long as the business of life and death is pursued in a dilettante fashion, the crucifixes can stay up there on the wall.

Chapter 12

The sense of possibility

The ball, the earthly globe, spins in the cosmos; *rien ne va plus*. If you are the Son of God then come down from the cross.[1] One miracle more or less shouldn't be a problem. But he stays where he is. *Rien ne va plus*.

For as long as the ball spins the players think of winning. Especially when after this there'll be no further play. We only live once. 'All may be well', says Shakespeare's Hamlet, expressing his sense of possibility.

The end brings gain, says Jesus: 'Look up and raise your heads, because your redemption is drawing near.'[2]

But not without risk;[3] we have only one chance, red or black, equal or unequal: 'Then two men will be in the field; one is taken and one is left. Two women will be grinding at the mill; one is taken and one is left'.

Where there is risk, thought and speech express a sense of possibility: I could win, perhaps I shall win, let us hope I shall win.

The fourth chapter of Robert Musil's *The Man without Qualities* is headed: 'If there is such a thing as a sense of reality, there must also be a sense of possibility.' 'Anyone possessing it', Musil says, 'does not say, for instance: here this or that has happened, will happen, must happen. He uses his imagination and says here such and such might, should or ought to happen. And if he is told that something *is* the way it is, then he thinks: well, it could probably just as easily be some other way. So the sense of possibility might be defined outright as the capacity to think how everything could "just as easily be," and to attach no more importance to what is than to what is not.'[4]

These concepts, it may now be said, adequately describe the impulse that led to the writing of this book. My object was to undertake an exercise in this style of thought without thereby suffering a loss of reality. To Jesus, something real signified no more than something imagined. It is he who gives the new possibilities their meaning and their direction, and it is he who raises them in the first place.

What Musil wanted to say in his – uncompleted – novel is thrown into relief through the agency of outsider characters:[5] the main character, Ulrich, stands in ironic aloofness from reality, and his further development is determined by his incest-relationship with his sister Agathe.

One should also notice that Musil thought of two other titles, *The Spy* and *The Redeemer*, before giving his novel the title by which we now know it. Furthermore, observe the title of the third volume: 'Into the Millennium (The Criminals).'

Musil comments: 'One ought really to become a forger [spy].' – 'People will say that this book is concerned only with the pettier variants of human behaviour.' – 'The only choice one has is between joining the others in their wretched expense of time [howling with the wolves], or becoming a neurotic.' – 'Had Ulrich lived at the time when the German nation was broken between Reformation and Counter-Reformation, he would most certainly have been neither Catholic nor Protestant.'[6]

Musil was working towards an end result. The debate carried on with reality by those who have a feeling for the possible passes on into the Utopian, including Musil's Utopia of inductive thought or of the given social situation. But of course Musil's thoughts on this matter, scattered about the novel, need to be read with an open mind; for instance, Chapter 116, to which Musil gave the heading: 'The two trees of life and the demand for a General Secretariat for Precision and the Spirit.'[7] I do not want to enter into further detail here.

According to Musil, 'Utopian ideas amount to more or less the same as possibilities. The fact that a possibility is not reality means nothing else than that the circumstances with which it is at present interwoven are preventing it from being so; for otherwise, of course, it would merely be an impossibility. If, however, the possibility is freed from its bonds and allowed to develop, the Utopian idea arises.'[8]

There is no doubt but that Jesus was a Utopian. Because the circumstances that hindered his sense of possibility are still effective today he was described as a social outsider.

Characterizing Jesus as an outsider is done with the help of a sense of reality that takes the form of common sense and the scientific attitude. Because, in fact, a sense of reality made little headway with Jesus, it banished him to the sphere that has always been reserved for unsettled questions of this sort, namely religion. This rendered Jesus harmless: in the Church he was free to do as he pleased and everyone else could get on with their jobs undisturbed. For as long as Jesus sticks to religion, steel production, population levels, and the power industry will get what they want without him. The Pope gives progress his blessing, and life goes on.

That in spite of all this Jesus has not yet finally disappeared is attributable to the fact that never before have so many possibilities been open to us. Without a sense of possibility even the wheel wouldn't have been discovered. The indicative alone does not make for a healthy language.

So let's have a look at the subjunctive mood: the indicative will look after itself – though the society in which this postulate is true is not always the best.

The rule of a thousand years[9] (Latin *mille* = 1000, hence millenniarism)[10] is outlined in Revelation: 'They shall be priests of God and of Christ, and they shall reign with him a thousand years.'

But first the devil will be enchained as the embodiment of everything evil in the world: 'Then I saw an angel coming down from heaven, holding in his hand the key of the bottomless pit and a great chain. And he seized the dragon, that ancient serpent, who is the Devil and Satan, and bound him for a thousand years, and threw him into the pit, and shut it and sealed it over him, that he should deceive the nations no more, till the thousand years were ended.'

Jesus in bad company

That is a theme that has since been richly orchestrated, has given rise to an assortment of images, starting with the followers of one Montanus in the second century up to the efforts of some Italian farmers at the end of the nineteenth century.

The central point: everyone will work, there will be neither rich nor poor, all will be equal, everything will be held in common, and the fruits of the earth will be justly divided; brotherliness will rule the earth.

In the early Middle Ages, heretics and fanatics in the West were few in number. But from the eleventh century onward the sense of the possible waxed vigorously from the Brabant to Bohemia, from Calabria to Languedoc, assuming various and often unpleasant forms, some ascetic, but others involving wife-swopping, processions of flagellants, anabaptists, but always revolutionary, not just furtive dreamers.

Millenniarism is described as a sincere rejection of the present and evil world, as a passionate longing for another and better one; thisworldly, not otherworldly, it yearns for a peacefully ordered society and customarily has only the vaguest of ideas concerning the actual political realization of its goal. Determined by linguistic imagery of strong emotional influence it attracted followers among the lower classes, especially in overpopulated regions, and spread its message in times of famine, scarcity, and epidemic.

Millenniarism is peculiar to agrarian economies and it features in history in so far as modern revolutionary movements differ from it at least in that usually they have very precise notions of their aims with regard to political organization, tactics, and strategy. But millenniarism's total rejection of the present order lives on in all modern revolutionary theories as the most powerful driving force behind the actions they take in the interests of a better future.

We can see that the sense of possibility also has its history – and it's by no means finished yet.

'The possible, however, covers not only the dreams of nervously sensitive persons but also the not yet manifested intentions of God.'[11] Within the sense of possibility one can recognize a weak strain, namely that associated with fault-finders, dreamers, know-alls, grumblers, and so-called idealists. They all suffer from a sort of hopelessness that prevents them from understanding reality, so that in their case the absence of a sense of reality signifies a real failing.

That there is no escape from death we know from our sense of reality, and to pretend otherwise can only mislead, and cause trouble.

Jesus was no mixed-up intellectual.

If Jesus stands at the most extreme front of human possibilities, unused and in pristine condition, then this needs to be seen in conjunction with his lack of function. For particular purposes, for instance political ones, Jesus is often in demand. The attempt in certain temporal conditions to interpret Jesus conceptually need not necessarily be considered objectionable, even if – in view of the aforesaid – we cannot necessarily approve the customary definition of politics as the art of the possible – at least not in this context; for the definition entails a pragmatic attitude to things that, though inevitable for those in a position of power, will not do as a yardstick for those who would follow Jesus. As through practice they become more adept followers of Jesus, they are more likely to see themselves as social outsiders, not because to be one is a goal in itself, but simply as a result of their way of life: 'A disciple is not above his teacher.'[12]

There is no shortage of examples of such careers; later generations have turned these extraordinary men into objects of veneration, thus rendering them – for instance as patron saints – largely harmless as stimuli for comparable efforts.

Yet it would be wrong to imagine that one would be beginning all over again were one to show interest in Jesus. Since his day, many attempts have been made to realize his initiatives – many of them shortlived, others of more enduring significance. Whether or not one reacts favourably to them, these attempts to achieve Jesus's objectives in the most varied social contexts represent an important body of experience, not all of which is useless.

Seen in this light, there is much in the Christian past that is yet

Jesus in bad company

to emerge from the cocoon; that the followers of Jesus would achieve yet greater works than he did – as John's gospel promises[13] – is not easy to see (as an already fulfilled promise) in history.

If it is nevertheless supposed to be good for us that Jesus should go away, as John's gospel puts it,[14] then a knowledge of Jesus based exclusively on history will not get us far, and nowhere at all when it presents him as a finished reality. Instead, one would suggest a knowledge that urges onward the process Jesus started, in other words a knowledge that travels his way.

The decision as to whether in effect Jesus did little more than launch a chimera, or whether, rather, his ideas are quite simply unborn realities, cannot be forced by proof. The best that the arguments and thoughts in this book can do is create an open space in which this decision can be made – a considered decision, of course, but one that when made is made boldly.

Notes

I. AN AMAZING LIFE STORY

1 Dionysius Exiguus (d. *c.* 550) produced several books on the calendar and was the first to reckon the years from Christ's birth; but he miscalculated by a few years.
2 In *The Sacred Mushroom and the Cross* (London, 1970), John M. Allegro defended the thesis that Jesus never lived but instead was a secret symbol for a hallucinogenic mushroom called *Amanita muscaria* used by the early Christians in their (orgiastic) rites.
3 Matt. 3:13; Mark 1:9; Luke 3:23; John 1:28f.
4 John 7:15.
5 Luke 2:41–52.
6 Cf. Talcott Parsons, *Societies – Evolutionary and Comparative Perspectives* (Englewood Cliffs, New Jersey, 1966), p. 102.
7 In *Jesus-Report* (Düsseldorf, 1970), Johannes Lehmann argued Jesus's total independence of the doctrines of the Qumran sect, though he is not supported in this view by unanimity among the experts.
8 In his book, *Was Jesus Married?* (1970), William E. Phipps presents an exhaustive discussion of this question. His view is that Jesus was married, though it must be noted that the presentation of his case is not strictly speaking scientific.
9 Matt. 1:1–17; Luke 3:23–38.
10 Mark 1:15.
11 The experts will concede the authenticity of a gospel saying or address attributed to Jesus only after the most thorough critical investigation; the number of authenticated sayings is relatively small.
12 Cf. Joachim Wach, *Religionssoziologie* (Tübingen, 1951), p. 387.
13 Matt. 16:28; Mark 13:26.
14 Matt. 25:5.
15 Karl Jaspers, *The Great Philosophers* (London, 1962), vol. I, p. 90.
16 Elias Canetti, *Crowds and Power* (London, 1962), p. 467.
17 Matt. 27:40.
18 Cf. Werner Harenberg, *Jesus und die Kirchen* (Stuttgart, 1966), p. 174.
19 John 8:58.
20 Søren Kierkegaard, *Philosophical fragments* (Princeton, 1967), pp. 124f.

Notes

2. CRIMINAL BEHAVIOUR

1 Luke 22:37.
2 Acts 8:32; cf. Isa. 53:7f.
3 Acts 3:17.
4 Matt. 27:25.
5 John 10:20; Mark 3:21.
6 Luke 7:36–50.
7 Luke 10:7.
8 Luke 5:33.
9 Luke 7:34.
10 Mark 2:15–17.
11 Luke 19:10.
12 Luke 5:34.
13 Matt. 22:9f.
14 Mark 3:1–6.
15 Matt. 5:33–37.
16 Cf. Robert K. Merton, *et al.*, *Sociology Today* (New York, 1959), p. 464.
17 Ernst Bloch, *Das Prinzip Hoffnung* (Frankfurt, 1959), p. 1490.
18 Rev. 21:5.
19 Ludwig Wittgenstein, *Tractatus Logico-philosophicus* (London, 1961), 6.52, p. 149.
20 John 19:7.

3. JESUS OR CHRIST

1 Bloch, *Das Prinzip Hoffnung*, p. 1487.
2 Cf. Peter L. Berger, *Rumour of Angels* (London, 1970), Chapter 1.
3 Mark 8:34; John 8:2; Mark 10:17–22.
4 John 6:68.
5 Kierkegaard, *Philosophical Fragments*, pp. 19f.; 111ff.; 130–1.
6 Erik H. Erikson, *Young Man Luther* (London, 1959).
7 Erikson, op. cit., pp. 134, 207.
8 Sigmund Freud, *Totem and Taboo* (London, 1950), p. 154.
9 1 Cor. 1:23.
10 According to N. H. Baynes, *Constantine the Great and the Christian Church* (London, 1931).
11 Arnold J. Toynbee, *A Study of History* (London, 1934), vol. II, Chapter V.
12 Max Scheler, *Die Wissensformen und die Gesellschaft* (Berne, 1960), p. 73.
13 Elias Canetti, *Crowds and Power*, p. 157.
14 G. Lindzey, *Handbook of Social Psychology* (Reading, Mass., 1954), pp. 164, 1044.

15 Bloch, *Das Prinzip Hoffnung*, pp. 1486f.
16 The expression comes from John's passion narrative (19:5) and means 'behold the man'.
17 Rev. 22:20; Luke 21:28.
18 1 Thess. 4:13–18.
19 Elias Canetti, *Crowds and Power*, p. 154.
20 Karl Jaspers, *The Great Philosophers*, p. 95.
21 Cf. Albert Camus, *L'homme révolté* (Paris, 1951), p. 52 (the only English translation of this book, *The Rebel* (London, 1951), is incomplete).

4. I HAVE NOT DWELT IN A HOUSE

1 John 4:5–26. Whether or not this story is historically reliable need not be discussed here.
2 2 Sam. 7:6.
3 Gen. 4.
4 Gen. 3:22.
5 Goethe, *Faust*, Part Two, Act 5.
6 Gen. 28:10–19.
7 Because of Jesus's descent from the tribe of David the town may have been important to the early Christians – cf. pp. 65f.
8 Matt. 21:13; the quotation is from Isa. 56:7.
9 Matt. 21:12–17; Mark 11:15–19; Luke 19:45f.; John 2:14–16. Amos 5:22; Hos. 4:4; 6:6; Matt. 9:13; Isa. 1:11–20.
10 Jer. 7:22.
11 Luke 7:16.
12 Heb. 7:14. For the (unknown) author of this doctrinal letter Jesus is also the one, true high priest; cf. 4:14 – 5:10.
13 Matt. 26:3; John 18:13f.
14 1 Pet. 2:5; Rev. 1:6.
15 Luke 10:31.
16 Matt. 8:4.
17 Matt. 26:61; John 2:19.
18 Mark 13:2. In Jesus's day, Jerusalem's population was about 70,000. Many people made their living from the temple trade brought through pilgrims. Cf. Joachim Jeremias, *Jerusalem in the time of Jesus* (London, 1969).
19 Matt. 17:24–27.
20 Luke 2:34; Matt. 21:42.
21 Acts 6 and 7.
22 John 7:37.
23 Their opposition to the temple worship in Jerusalem stems from calendar disputes; cf. Schubert, *Kulturgeschichte*, pp. 169f.

Notes

24 Rev. 21:22.
25 Matt. 27:51; Mark 15:38; Luke 23:45.

5. NOLI ME TANGERE

1 John 20:11–18.
2 S. of S. 3:4.
3 Matt. 19:5; Mark 10:7; the quotation is from Gen. 2:24.
4 Luke 2:4.
5 Matt. 13:53–58; Mark 6:1–6; Luke 4:16–24; John 4:44.
6 Cf. J. Prytz-Johansen, *The Maori and his Religion* (Copenhagen, 1954), p. 9.
7 Claude Lévi-Strauss, *Totemism* (London, 1964), p. 141.
8 John 1:45.
9 Mark 3:31–35; Luke 8:19–21.
10 Luke 2:41–50.
11 Karl Jaspers, *The Great Philosophers*, p. 88.
12 The story is taken from Otto Karrer, *Franz von Assisi. Legenden und Laude* (Zurich, 1945), pp. 47f.
13 Luke 11:27f.
14 John 2:4; 19:26.
15 John 7:25–29; 40: 43.
16 *The Confessions of St Augustine* (Penguin edition, Harmondsworth, 1961), p. 170.
17 *Confessions*, pp. 175–6.
18 *Confessions*, p. 176.
19 *Confessions*, p. 234.
20 Matt. 19:12; debate still continues about the authenticity of this saying.
21 Luke 20:34.
22 Matt. 24:38f.
23 Luke 14:26.
24 Luke 12:51–53.
25 Matt. 10:37.
26 Matt. 10:36.
27 Matt. 19:1–10 (cf. 5:32); Mark 10:1–12.
28 Catholic exegetes still consider this a matter of dispute, presumably because they are concerned to protect the doctrine of the virgin birth; they therefore refer to Jesus's male and female cousins.
29 Pseudo-Clement and the Gospel of Thomas rank as so-called apocryphal writings. These two examples appear to be very old and stem therefore from the very early days of Christianity. However, they were never included within the official Christian Bible. Cf. *New Testament Apocrypha* (London, 1950).
30 As early as the Middle Ages the sale of Church property was subject to severe restrictions and thus such property only rarely changed

hands (it was therefore known as *manus mortua* (dead hand)). The increase in such goods (*admortisatio* – from whence the modern word amortization) was a matter of concern to emperors and princes as early as the ninth century.

31 Cf. Carl Gustav Jung, *Psychology and Religion: West and East* (London, 1970), p. 461–2.
32 Erik H. Erikson, *Young Man Luther*, p. 68.
33 2 Cor. 11:2; Rev. 21:9; C. G. Jung, loc. cit.
34 John 1:13.
35 Luke 12:49.
36 Luke 16:18; Matt. 5:27–30; cf. Mark 9:43–48.
37 John 7:53 – 8:11.
38 Karl Jaspers, *The Great Philosophers*, p. 78.
39 1 Cor. 7.
40 Cf. Alfred C. Kinsey, *Sexual Behaviour in the Human Male* (London, 1958), p. 469.
41 Karl Kraus, *Auswahl aus dem Werk* (Frankfurt, 1961), p. 26.
42 R. S. Lee, *Freud and Christianity* (Harmondsworth, 1967), pp. 146–52.
43 Robert Musil, *The Man without Qualities* (London, 1953), vol. I, p. 12.
44 Mark 3:21.

6. THE DOWNWARD TENDENCY

1 François Villon, *Complete Poems*, 'The Last Will and Testament' (London, 1968).
2 Jaspers, *The Great Philosophers*, p. 91.
3 Bloch, *Das Prinzip Hoffnung*, p. 1482.
4 Luke 2:22–24.
5 Matt. 11:8.
6 Luke 6:20f.
7 Max Weber, *Gesammelte Aufsätze zur Religionssoziologie* (Tübingen, 1966), pp. 37, 44, 74, 407–10.
8 Matt. 7:29.
9 Matt. 6:21; Luke 12:34.
10 Matt. 11:25; Luke 10:21.
11 Weber, *Gesammelte Aufsätze*, pp. 409, 419.
12 Luke 14:8–11.
13 Matt. 11:5; cf. Isa. 61:1.
14 Mark 10:31.
15 Luke 11:20.
16 Luke 11:2f.
17 Matt. 6:34.
18 Luke 12:16–20.
19 Matt. 6:19, 28f., 33.

20 Ernst Bloch, *Atheismus im Christentum* (Frankfurt, 1968), p. 184.
21 Arnold Toynbee, *A Study of History*, vol. 1, pp. 147ff.
22 Cf. Eric J. Hobsbawm, *Primitive Rebels* (Manchester, 1959), p. 183; p. 74 (the Spanish anarchists).
23 Mark 13:2.
24 Rudolf Bultmann, *Primitive Christianity* (London, 1956); quoted from the Fontana paperback edition (London, 1960), p. 246.
25 Matt. 27:63.
26 Luke 23:5.
27 John 7:12.
28 Matt. 15:32; Mark 8:1 (multiplying the loaves). Cf. Mark 6:34.
29 Matt. 11:21–24; Luke 10:13–15. – Luke 13:34 (Jerusalem).
30 Matt. 11:16f.; Luke 7:31–35.
31 John 6:26.
32 Matt. 4:4.; Luke 4:4. The quotation is from Deut. 8:3.
33 Matt. 25:40.
34 Bloch, *Atheismus im Christentum*, p. 186.
35 Luke 10:37.
36 Mark 10:17–22; Luke 12:33.
37 Matt. 23:12.
38 Matt. 18:2–4.
39 Matt. 11:28–30.
40 Luke 14:13.
41 Cf. Arno Plack, *Die Gesellschaft und das Böse* (Munich, 1969), pp. 110, 317.
42 Ps. 77:31 (in the Latin translation of the Vulgate).
43 The theory of the priestly betrayal was developed by Dietrich von Holbach (d. 1789).
44 Cf. Paul A. Samuelson, *Economics* (New York, 1967), Chapter 6.
45 Luke 12:32.
46 Luke 11:29.
47 Matt. 8:20; Luke 9:58.
48 Matt. 21:31.
49 Luke 15.
50 Luke 18:9–14.
51 Cf. Weber, *Gesammelte Aufsätze*, p. 403.
52 John 8:48.
53 Luke 10:29–37.
54 Matt. 18:23–35.
55 Luke 7:11–17.
56 Luke 7:35; Matt. 5:44–47.
57 A sociogram is a sociometric diagram representing the pattern of relationships between individuals in a group, usually expressed in terms of which persons they prefer to associate with.

7. THE VERY STONES WOULD CRY OUT

1 Matt. 21:1–11; Mark 11:1–11; Luke 19:28–38; John 12:12–16.
2 Jer. 15:10–17.
3 Eric J. Hobsbawm, see note 22, Chapter 6.
4 Cf. Jaspers, *The Great Philosophers*, pp. 82–3.
5 Luke 12:49.
6 Matt. 10:34.
7 Luke 9:62.
8 Matt. 8:22.
9 Erikson, *Young Man Luther*, p. 145.
10 Rev. 3:16.
11 Luke 1:46–55.
12 Job 12:18.
13 Bloch, *Das Prinzip Hoffnung*, p. 576.
14 Hos. 9:15; cf. 1 Sam. 8:5; 11:15.
15 Elijah and Elisha: cf. Kurt Schubert, *Handbuch der Kulturgeschichte* (Frankfurt, 1970), pp. 96f.
16 Mark 9:2–10.
17 Weber, *Gesammelte Aufsätze*, p. 125.
18 Ibid., p. 285.
19 Jer. 15:15.
20 Parsons, *Societies*, p. 101.
21 Isa. 2:4; 11:6f.
22 Weber, *Gesammelte Aufsätze*, p. 249.
23 Luke 7:16; cf. Matt. 13:57; 16:14; Mark 6:15; John 4:19.
24 Cf. Kurt Niederwimmer, *Jesus* (Göttingen, 1968), p. 28.
25 Canetti, *Crowds and Power*, pp. 15, 204, 206, 303, 304, 305.
26 Jaspers, *The Great Philosophers*, p. 83.
27 Mark 13:28f.; Luke 12:54–56.
28 Cf. Schubert, *Kulturgeschichte*, pp. 190, 198.
29 Luke 6:15. Cf. Oscar Cullmann, *Jesus und die Revolutionäre seiner Zeit* (Tübingen, 1970), pp. 22f.
30 Bultmann, *Primitive Christianity*, p. 102.
31 Cf. Toynbee, *A Study of History*, vol. I. Toynbee lists a series of Egyptian uprisings against the Ptolemaic dictatorship; the Jewish revolts; uprisings in western Asia Minor between 132 and 88 BC; uprisings of slaves in Sicily and southern Italy reaching their highpoint from 73–71 BC (Spartacus); and troubles in Rome from 91–82 BC.
32 Luke 12:4.
33 Canetti, *Crowds and Power*, p. 470.
34 Marx, *The Economic and Philosophic Manuscripts of 1844* (New York, 1966), p. 138.
35 Rom. 6:9. Cf. 1 Cor. 15:54–57.
36 Canetti, *Crowds and Power*, pp. 227f.

Notes

37 Weber, *Gesammelte Aufsätze*, p. 418.
38 Bultmann, *Primitive Christianity*, p. 51
39 Isa. 55:8.
40 Canetti, *Crowds and Power*, p. 298.
41 Gen. 3. Cf. Bloch, *Atheismus im Christentum*, pp. 102–25, 231–7.
42 Camus, *L'homme révolté*, p. 51.
43 Job 1:21; 9:19; 9:22f.; 10:1; 12:16; 38:4; 42:10.
44 Canetti, *Crowds and Power*, p. 298.
45 Cf. C. G. Jung, *Psychology and Religion: West and East*, p. 369.
46 Jaspers, *The Great Philosophers*, p. 132.
47 Mark 14:64.
48 Niederwimmer, *Jesus*, p. 55.
49 Quoted by Bultmann, *Primitive Christianity*, p. 76.
50 Luke 24:27.
51 Niederwimmer, *Jesus*, p. 55.
52 Camus: see note 21, Chapter 3.
53 Matt. 7:9–11.
54 Matt. 5:29f.
55 Matt. 10:28.
56 Jaspers, *The Great Philosophers*, p. 84.
57 Cf. 1 Cor. 5:7; Eph. 5:2. The classical passage on original sin is Rom. 5:12–21. Cf. Herbert Haag, *Biblische Schöpfungslehre und kirchliche Erbsündenlehre* (Stuttgart, 1966).
58 Niederwimmer, *Jesus*, pp. 32–5.
59 Mark 3:22.
60 Cf. Lindzey, *Handbook of Social Psychology*, p. 164.
61 G. van der Leeuw, *Phänomenologie der Religion* (Tübingen, 1956), p. 148.
62 Friedrich Heiler, *Erscheinungsformen und Wesen der Religion* (Stuttgart, 1961), p. 315.
63 Van der Leeuw, *Phänomenologie der Religion*, p. 141.
64 Mark 1:22.
65 Mark 3:22–27.
66 Luke 10:18.
67 Mark 2:27.
68 Matt. 12:11f.
69 Not all the gospel accounts of the dispute between Jesus and the Pharisees can be regarded as authentic; sometimes they reflect disputes between the early Christians and the Pharisees. Cf. Schubert, *Kulturgeschichte*, p. 199.
70 Cf. Lindzey, *Handbook of Social Psychology*, pp. 136, 247–50, 1045.
71 Bertolt Brecht, *Der Jasager und der Neinsager* (Frankfurt, 1967), p. 49.
72 Cf. Michael Argyle, *Psychology and Social Problems* (London, 1967), p. 30.

73 Canetti, *Crowds and Power*, p. 306.
74 Matt. 22:21.
75 Mark 10:42-44.
76 Erikson, *Young Man Luther*, p. 145.

8. I CALL YOU FRIENDS

1 1 Cor. 11:24f. Cf. Matt. 26:26-29; Mark 14:22-25; Luke 22:14-20. These so-called sacramental words, or words of institution, still constitute the heart of Christian worship celebrated by Catholics as the Mass and by Protestants as the Communion Service.
2 Cf. Niederwimmer, *Jesus*, p. 73.
3 Acts 2:42-46.
4 John 13:1.
5 Cf. Rudolf Schnackenburg, *The Gospel of St John*, vol. I (London, 1968).
6 John 21:3-5.
7 John 1:35-39.
8 Wach, *Religionssoziologie*, p. 151.
9 Jaspers, *The Great Philosophers*, p. 100.
10 Cf. Heinz Schürmann, *Das Lukasevangelium*, vol. I (Freiburg, 1969), pp. 314-16. Schürmann argues for the historicity of the twelve as a 'messianic sign'; other exegetes are less certain on this point.
11 Acts 1:21f.
12 Acts 1:15.
13 1 Cor. 15:6.
14 Luke 8:2f.; 23:49, 55f.; Acts 1:14.
15 Mark 5:25-34.
16 John 11:5.
17 Luke 10:38-42.
18 John 11:36.
19 John 13:23; 19:26; 20:2.
20 John 15:15.
21 G. W. F. Hegel, *Phenomenology of Mind* (London, 1931), vol. I, pp. 234-40.
22 John 13:13-15.
23 John 13:2-12.
24 John 15:13.
25 G. W. F. Hegel, *Der Geist des Christentums und sein Schicksal* (Gütersloh, 1970), p. 72.
26 John 3:3-5.
27 John 15:12.
28 Hegel, *Der Geist des Christentums*, p. 78.
29 Acts 4:32-34; 2:47.

Notes

30 Acts 5:29.
31 Acts 9:1–9.
32 Acts 9:31.
33 Acts 3:20; 5:30f.
34 Cf. Peter R. Hofstätter, *Einführung in die Sozialpsychologie* (Stuttgart, 1959), pp. 307–11.
35 John 1:1–17.
36 John 17:9.
37 Bloch, *Atheismus im Christentum*, p. 188.

9. TRANSLATION DIFFICULTIES

1 Benjamin Lee Whorf, *Language, Thought and Reality* (M.I.T., 1956).
2 For example, Mark 5:41 (*talita kum*).

10. THE CIRCUMSTANCE OF PLACE

1 Plato, *Theaetetus*, §149. Cf. Kierkegaard, *Philosophical Fragments*, p. 13.
2 Matt. 27:37; Mark 15:26; Luke 23:38; John 19:19–22.
3 Mark 13:9.
4 2 Cor. 11:23.
5 Heb. 11:37.
6 Matt. 5:11f.
7 Augustine, *Confessions*, p. 317.
8 Matt. 13:45f.
9 Mark 11:23.
10 Luke 23:43.
11 Matt. 18:3.
12 Cf. Hobsbawm, *Primitive Rebels*, pp. 113f.
13 See p. 143.

11. THE CIRCUMSTANCE OF TIME

1 Eccles. 1:2.
2 Matt. 16:18.
3 1 Cor. 7:31.
4 Matt. 26:64.
5 Samuel Beckett, *Endgame* (London, 1970), p. 12.
6 Matt. 24:42; 25:13; Mark 13:33–37; Luke 12:35–40; Rev. 3:2f. Cf. Isa. 21:11f.
7 Matt. 9:37f.; Luke 21:30; John 4:34–38; Rev. 14:14–19.
8 John 16:21.
9 Beckett, *Endgame*, p. 48.

10 Cf. the book of this title by Oswald Spengler (London, 1932).
11 John 19:30.

12. THE SENSE OF POSSIBILITY

1 Matt. 27:40.
2 Luke 21:28.
3 Matt. 24:40; Luke 17:34.
4 Musil, *The Man without Qualities*, p. 12.
5 Outsider figures: Ulrich's counterpart, Arnheim (behind whom hides the true Rathenau), may be interpreted as the man of reality – successful and well adapted. Clarisse and Moosbrugger represent madness and crime. Other individuals among whom Ulrich moves without attaching himself to any of them represent the traditional social forces: Stumm von Bordwehr (the army); Leinsdorf, Tuzzi (politics); Fischel (finance); Walter and Diotima (culture); Lindner and Hagauer (education); Ulrich's father (law).
6 Musil, *Der Mann ohne Eigenschaften*, pp. 1574, 1578–84, 1591, 1594f. The last fragmentary sections of Musil's *Man without Qualities* have not yet been translated.
7 Musil, *The Man without Qualities*, vol. 2, p. 348.
8 Musil, *The Man without Qualities*, vol. 1, p. 292.
9 Rev. 20:1–6.
10 Cf. Norman Cohn, *The Pursuit of the Millennium* (London, 1970).
11 Musil, *The Man without Qualities*, p. 16.
12 Matt. 10:24.
13 John 14:12; cf. Mark 16:17f.
14 John 16:7.

Acknowledgments

The Scripture quotations in this publication are from the Revised Standard Version of the Bible, copyrighted 1946 and 1952 by the Division of Christian Education of the National Council of the Churches of Christ in the USA, and used by permission. Quotations from St Augustine's *Confessions* are from the translation by R. S. Pine-Coffin, Copyright © R. S. Pine-Coffin, 1961, and are reproduced by kind permission of the publishers, Penguin Books Ltd.